In 100 Years

In 100 Years

Leading Economists Predict the Future

edited by Ignacio Palacios-Huerta

The MIT Press
Cambridge, Massachusetts
London, England

MIT Press books may be purchased at special quantity discounts for business or sales promotional use. For information, please email special_sales@mitpress.mit.edu.

This book was set in Stone Serif and Stone Sans by the MIT Press. Printed and bound in the United States of America.

Library of Congress Cataloging-in-Publication Data
In 100 years : leading economists predict the future / edited by Ignacio Palacios-Huerta.
   p.   cm
Includes bibliographical references and index.
ISBN 978-0-262-02691-8 (hardcover : alk. paper)
1. Economic development—Forecasting. I. Palacios-Huerta, Ignacio. II. Title: In one hundred years.
HD82.I2985   2013
330.9001'12—dc23
2013025303

10 9 8 7 6 5 4 3 2 1

To Ana, Ander, and Julene
To Jose Antonio, Mª Luz, Javi, Patxo, Antton, and Jon

Contents

10   The Geoengineered Planet   145
Martin L. Weitzman

Acknowledgments

My deep thanks go first to each of the chapter authors for the gift of their chapter. They have decided to use their time, human capital, and intuition in a most laudable way: to argue, write, debate, and speak, as they have always done—in this case about a question that I hope you will find of the utmost interest. I cannot thank them enough for the pleasure of reading their views and analyses. Whether you are reading this book in 2013, 2063, or 2113, I hope you will find their essays a true gift as much as I do.

Second, I thank John S. Covell at MIT Press, who enthusiastically supported this project from the very beginning.

Finally, I thank my wife, Ana, and my children, Ander and Julene, for their love and for giving me a life I never dreamed of. My mother, my late father, and my brothers also deserve the same thanks. I am sure the idea for this book would have never occurred to me without the love, support, and environment they have always provided.

The Idea for *In 100 Years*

Ignacio Palacios-Huerta

In *An Enquiry Concerning Human Understanding*, published in 1748, the Scottish philosopher David Hume reduced the principles of associative memory—in which each idea is linked to many others in a network—down to three: resemblance, contiguity in time and place, and causality. I do not remember exactly how the idea for this book appeared in my mind, but Hume's principles provide good guidance. I have three suspects. The first are my twin children. When they were born eight and a half years ago, I started thinking about the future with much greater care and intensity than before. Before their birth, my thinking about the future was mostly "scientific" (as in the economics literature on human capital investments that pay off in one's lifetime or in the literature about how one day in the far future, the sun will run out of fuel and end its life). When they were born, however, I started thinking with much greater precision about the next ten to twenty years (e.g., what school and neighborhood would be most appropriate for them, which foreign languages they should learn, and so on). True, this is not the future in 100 years, but it is something along that line. The second suspect is perhaps more difficult to express in simple words: it is the perception, the deeply and fundamentally sad perception, that my life is going to end. All of us know that this life is finite, of course, but the unbearable awareness that it will end *for sure*, which in my case has been patently obvious only recently, particularly in the dark early hours, made me wonder about the more distant future only in the past few years. How will this world look when I am not here? Will there be other world wars? Will the ice poles melt? Will poverty as we know it today disappear? What will my great-great-grandchildren be like? Will the human race have begun planning to move to another planet as physicist Stephen Hawking is suggesting today? Will . . . ? How will . . . ? When will . . . ? I am so curious.

The third suspect is the 1930 essay by John Maynard Keynes, "Economic Possibilities for Our Grandchildren," which I read recently. Published in his book *Essays in Persuasion* as the Great Depression was beginning, Keynes looks 100 years ahead to a time in which learning to live well had replaced the struggle for subsistence. He makes a number of interesting predictions. Some of them turned out to be absolutely correct, for example, living standards would be between four and eight times higher, and some spectacularly wrong, for example, a working week cut to around fifteen hours per week (I know, it is not 2030 yet!).

I do not know for sure, but if I had to guess, I believe the combination of these three ingredients installed in my mind the question: "What will the world look like in 100 years?" Once it appeared, it was hard to stop thinking about it. It was an unusually difficult and interesting question—perhaps even an important one, and not just to me but potentially to thousands and millions of other people. At first I tried to give myself a few answers, which I will not venture to write down now. After a few minutes, my demand for knowledge increased by an order of magnitude: "What would Mr. X and Mr. Y think? How about Mr. Z and Ms. W? What would they say? How do they imagine 'the future'?" I thought it would be great to know. So at that moment I strongly felt this was a book that *had* to be written and that it was my responsibility that it be written.

I was certain that the specific people X, Y, Z, and W I first had in mind would agree that it was an original, difficult, and attractive question. And so when the thought that they and others might find it uninteresting or ridiculous crossed my mind, I quickly dismissed it. In any event, just to make sure, I first mentioned the idea to a few close friends. When I saw that it was enthusiastically received, I became strongly encouraged to pursue the project of this book. Then I contacted John S. Covell at MIT Press (the publisher of *Revisiting Keynes*, a book in which a number of authors analyze Keynes's 1930 essay). He was also enthusiastic about the idea and immediately said that MIT Press would be interested in publishing it. The last step was to ask the question to X, Y, Z, and W and see if in fact they were interested and had the time to write an essay with their predictions for the next 100 years. My plan was to edit a book with just about ten to twelve chapters by people I like, find insightful and interesting, and who have different backgrounds and fields of research expertise. And so I started with some invitations hoping that I was not overly optimistic about this project.

I was not. The reaction was excellent and the vast majority accepted the invitation immediately. For instance:

Hi Ignacio: to my surprise, I do find your invitation tempting. It's a sign of old age, I'm afraid. Count me in: I'll be happy to try to predict the far future . . .

Al Roth

or

Dear Ignacio, It is good to hear from you after all these years. Making predictions in the secure knowledge that one will not have to see them tested is a temptation one should resist. But, at least tentatively, I don't plan to resist. However, given my background in statistics, I would undoubtedly give error bands or at least alternative scenarios. Put me down as a yes.

Yours, Ken Arrow

Even people who politely declined had good words to say about it:

After reflecting on it for several days, I am not sure I have enough confidence in my views on this matter to share them so publicly. But I appreciate your thinking of me, and I look forward to reading the book!

Others declined with interesting thoughts:

Dear Ignacio: My answer to your kind and thoughtful invitation is that I do not predict the future. Rather, I try to understand the past. I am an economic historian, not a fortune teller. I know that the big money is in prediction. But that is not what I do. Best of luck with this project. Regards

Unfortunately, there were some, such as Kenneth Arrow, Gary Becker, and Robert Fogel, who, after having accepted the invitation, had to decline because personal matters did not allow them to complete their contribution before the publishing deadline. Too bad; really bad.

In the end, it is a true honor for me to be the editor of this book. In many ways, it summarizes the best of what some of the best social scientists of the twentieth century have learned during a century of unprecedented advances in our understanding of the economic, social, and political environment. Their knowledge and educated intuition about the mechanics of the economy, development, the environment, institutions, human nature, and so many other aspects of our life in this planet is used in their chapters to predict what awaits us in the future. How correct their predictions will be is, of course, an empirical question. Predictions, especially so far in the future, are always difficult. The twentieth century would have probably been quite different if the Academy of Fine Arts in Vienna had not rejected Adolf Hitler as "unfit for painting" or if Joseph Stalin's promising career as a poet had been given a serious chance. And my Basque Country would have been quite different if Franco had died in the Rif War.

We all know that what economists do to "show" us the future, particularly the distant future, is definitely not as emotionally attractive as what literary people can achieve in their writing or as visually attractive as the work of some filmmakers. For instance, the hypnotic film *Blade Runner* (1982) comes to mind with its seamless portrait of the future, where overcrowded cities are roamed by hustlers and gangs muttering a multicultural dialect, with the sky lit by giant video billboards advertising getaways on other planets. A movie with a description of the future like that, and similar ones in other sci-fi movies, is so visually convincing and attractive to most people that it is impossible for any economist to beat.

But economists, at least some economists, are much better equipped to make predictions than movie makers and other scientists. This does not make them infallible, of course. But they know more about the laws of human interactions and have reflected more deeply and with better methods than any other human beings. As difficult as it may be, I would bet that they are the ones more likely to be correct. In any event, if you are reading this collection of essays circa 2113, you should know that there was a general consensus back in 2013 that the chapter authors in this book were among the leading social scientists of their generation. If I had to make a prediction today, it is that every one of them will be awarded a Nobel Prize in Economics by 2113.

Finally, a famous speech by William Faulkner contained an idea that I think the manifold messages in this book develop with great intensity. It is probably suitable as a concluding quotation that points to the future: "I do not believe in the end of man," at least in the next 100 years.

1 The World Our Grandchildren Will Inherit

Daron Acemoglu

I write as I await the birth of my second son. If trends about fatherhood continue as they have over the past several decades, the chances are that he will have children in his forties, and (some of) my grandchildren will be in their forties or fifties in the year 2113. What sort of world will they inhabit? The track record of forecasts in social sciences does not inspire much confidence in our ability to predict events in the next 100 years. But prediction about the future is often a vehicle for clarifying the challenges ahead, and because it partly extrapolates from experience, it also gives us an opportunity to take stock of the trends that have shaped our age. It is in this spirit that I take on this task.

I start with what I believe are the ten most important trends that have defined our economic, social, and political lives over the past 100 years—though naturally there can be much disagreement on these. I then offer a framework for interpreting these trends. Finally, I use this framework to trace out what the next 100-year continuation of these trends might be.

Trend 1 The Rights Revolution

Ours has been the age of political rights. Figure 1.1 shows the evolution of two indexes of political rights and democracy, documenting this trend since both 1950 and the beginning of the twentieth century.[1] Never before in human history have so many people taken part in choosing their leaders and having at least some voice in how their societies are governed. And despite the doomsayers, it has not worked out too badly. Ortega y Gasset, though a liberal by inclination, raised the alarm bells at the beginning of the twentieth century, warning of the dangers of mass participation in politics in his *The Revolt of the Masses*. But to most other citizens in many parts of the world, most notably in western Europe and its offshoots, democratic political participation has become second nature, and for the most part, the masses have shown that they can have an intelligent voice in politics. We have witnessed with the Arab Spring a vibrant demand for democracy and its onset even in places where social scientists and pundits alike had ruled it out. Many still fear that the uneducated and easily manipulable masses cannot govern themselves and democracy is an unstable system at best, and thus they advocate that in practice, any democracy should be managed by responsible elites and political rights de facto limited. The American intellectual Walter Lippmann articulated this idea by writing: "The common interests very largely elude public opinion entirely, and can be managed only by a specialized class whose personal interests reach beyond the locality."[2]

These popular ideas—at least among the intellectual elite—notwithstanding, political rights for the less educated and less privileged have often brought policies that have redistributed resources or made public services

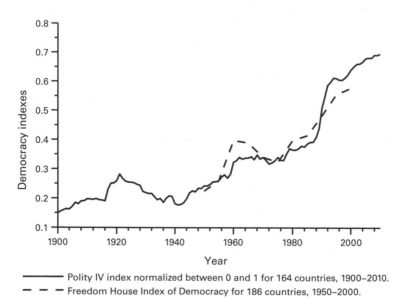

———— Polity IV index normalized between 0 and 1 for 164 countries, 1900–2010.
— — — Freedom House Index of Democracy for 186 countries, 1950–2000.

Figure 1.1
Democratization, 1900–2010

more widely available to them, even if the elites have sometimes resisted them. Recent research by Thomas Fujiwara provides one example of this from Brazil, exploiting the effective enfranchisement of the less educated whose ballots were often spoiled because of an antiquated and difficult voting system. Simplifying and automating the voting system led to a massive reduction in spoiled ballots, mostly by the less educated and poor voters. Fujiwara shows that this did lead to the election of mayors advocating more widespread redistribution, and it was no bad thing. These mayors were more likely to implement policies favoring these newly enfranchised voters, such as better health care delivery, which led to a significant drop in infant mortality.[3]

The spectacular advancement of rights has not been confined to political rights for the majority. The civil rights and freedoms of individuals, women, and (religious, ethnic, and sexual) minorities are much better protected throughout the world today than 100 years ago. A century ago, women did not have the vote and were discriminated against in law and in practice, and the situation was worse for sexual minorities. To name just one celebrated case, Oscar Wilde served a two-year prison sentence with hard labor for homosexuality in 1895. Overt discrimination and violence against women and ethnic minorities were not confined to places such as the Ottoman Empire and Russia; they were also commonplace in Europe and the United States (anti-Semitism being just one example).

This is not to suggest that the journey has not been a bumpy one. Fascism and other authoritarian forms of government reared their ugly heads on the way, including in Germany, Italy, Japan, and even in the United States. Aggressive nationalism and militarism have been much more widespread. And it has been an incomplete and partial revolution; the majority of the population today still lives under authoritarian forms of government. These governments often pursue policies that further the interests of a narrow elite rather than the population at large, and violation of the civil rights of women and minorities is much more likely in these authoritarian regimes for reasons I discuss below. Nevertheless, the rights revolution has so permeated the world we live in that even authoritarian regimes, ranging from China to Russia and Iran, are curtailed in what they can do, and they are often forced to moderate their repression of individuals, women, and minorities.

The unparalleled expansion of civil and political rights, though incomplete, is momentous not only because of its transformative impact on the lives of billions, but also because the other major trends are largely shaped by its trajectory and follow from it.

Trend 2   The Sweep of Technology

The Industrial Revolution brought forth a wave of new machines and improvements of technology in textiles, steam power, transport, metallurgy, and communications. But the pace at which new gadgets, techniques, and products has been introduced during the past century has easily surpassed that of the Industrial Revolution. In consequence, we now have access to technologies that would have been difficult for our great-grandparents to imagine; they include not only recent advances such as computer-assisted machinery and robots, the Internet, a whole array of new communication technologies, and social media, but also such things as breakthrough drugs and medical technologies, indoor plumbing, refrigerators and other household durables, much better and inexpensive lighting, radio, TV, inexpensive air and ground travel, and a huge increase in entertainment and culinary options. The impact of these technologies goes well beyond the organization of production, permeating every aspect of our social lives.

Trend 3   Unrelenting Growth

Underpinned by these technological breakthroughs, ours has also been the age of sustained economic growth. The nineteenth century also witnessed economic growth, but both its pace and its pervasiveness do not compare to the past 100 years. The average citizen of the world has much higher income than 100 years ago. Figure 1.2 depicts the average income per capita in the world economy over the past 200 years (in constant purchasing power parity, PPP, 2010 dollars). We are about eight times richer than our grandparents (or in fact great-grandparents) who lived at the beginning of the previous century.[4]

Figure 1.2 also plots the evolution of income per capita in two of the most advanced economies over this period, the United States and the United Kingdom, showing that in these leading economies, economic growth over the past 100 years has taken place in a relatively sustained and steady manner—the Great Depression notwithstanding.

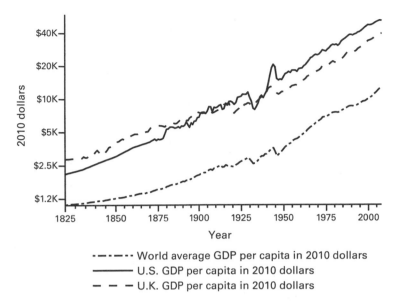

Figure 1.2
GDP per capita, 1825–2005

Trend 4   Uneven Growth

A remarkable fact is that the economic growth of our age has not been even. Although the world has become more integrated, the gap between rich and poor nations has widened by most measures. Figure 1.3 depicts the ratio between the 90th and 10th percentiles and between the 75th and 25th percentiles of the country-level income per capita distribution. It shows the gap between the very rich (90th percentile) and very poor (10th percentile) countries, as well as that between moderately rich and moderately poor (75th and 25th percentiles) opening up steadily over this time period. The 90th-to-10th percentile ratio was less than 9 at the beginning of the century and has increased to more than 30 today. If we go back to the middle of the nineteenth century, before the Industrial Revolution gained full steam and before Adam Smith set out to compose the *Wealth of Nations*, this gap was most likely less than 3.[5]

Figure 1.3 also shows that if we instead look at population-weighted numbers, the picture is more nuanced, with a decline in the ratio between the 90th and 10th percentiles over the past twenty years owing to the recent rapid growth of several populous nations such as Brazil, China, and India. All the same, the trends, which indicate an increase in the ratio between the 90th and the 10th percentiles of the country-level income distribution from less than 6 to almost 20 during the past century, would certainly have disappointed all but the most pessimistic forecasters weighing in on the economic possibilities for the vast majority of the world's population.

Trend 5   The Transformation of Work and Wages

Technological changes have also transformed the nature of work. In many advanced economies, agriculture was in relative decline already in the nineteenth century. The agricultural sector has continued to wane, but manufacturing, a key driver of the early stages of growth in many of these economies, has also started a secular decline, being replaced by the service sector. Agricultural employment has started a downward trend in less-developed economies as well.

Equally far reaching has been another aspect of the transformation of work in advanced economies: the disappearance of many of the middle-skill,

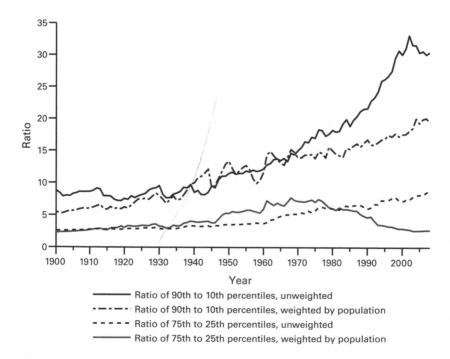

Figure 1.3
Uneven economic growth, 1900–2010

manual jobs—in particular, in the United States, Canada, western Europe, and Japan.[6] A complementary process, again unleashed by technological advances and contributing to the same outcomes, has been the globalization of technology and production: many tasks previously performed domestically by low- and middle-skill workers are now offshored to places such as China, where labor is cheaper. An important consequence of this trend has been distributional: as the demand for low- and middle-skill work has declined, the distribution of earnings has become more unequal, and as the middle-skill jobs have disappeared, it has become polarized. Figure 1.4 illustrates this by documenting a widening gap between the 90th and 10th percentiles, and especially between the 90th and the 50th percentiles, of the U.S. earnings distribution. Figure 1.5 shows the hollowing out of the income distribution by depicting how different percentiles of wages have change relative to the 90th percentile between 1970 and 2008.[7]

Trend 6   The Health Revolution

Although the wealth of nations has become more unequal—or at the very least stayed as highly unequal as it was at the beginning of the previous

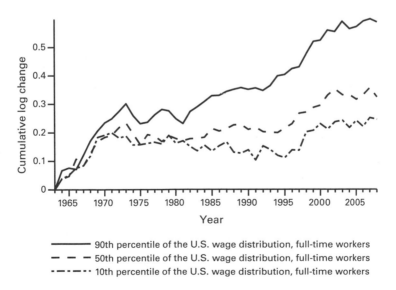

Figure 1.4
Evolution of the 10th, 50th, and 90th percentiles of the U.S. wage distribution, 1963–2008

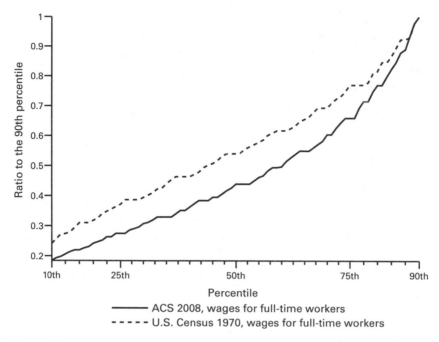

Figure 1.5
Distribution of wages in the United States

century—the picture is very different for the health of nations. Figure 1.6 shows the striking narrowing in differences in life expectancy over the past 100 years by plotting the evolution of life expectancy at birth for the whole world and separately for Europe and its offshoots (Australia, Canada, New Zealand, and the United States), Asia and Latin America, and sub-Saharan Africa.[8] Owing to the major health innovations and their diffusion throughout the world, even the poorest nations today enjoy health conditions unparalleled in the nineteenth century.

Trend 7   Technology without Borders

New communication technologies and changes in trade policies have also created a more integrated world. Though, as figure 1.7 shows, international trade as a fraction of national income was also high in the early twentieth century, the globalization of technology and production distinguishes the recent period.[9] Advances in communication technologies and possibilities

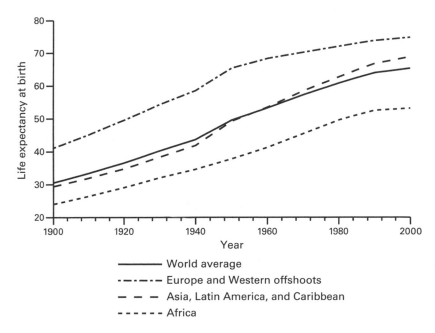

Figure 1.6
Convergence in life expectancy, 1900–2000

for outsourcing and offshoring tasks now enable firms to more comprehensively arbitrage low wages around the world. Besides its impact on wage inequality in advanced economies, this process has also enabled much more rapid growth in economies such as China, which has been able to leverage its abundant low-wage labor without having to go through the same investments and similar technological and institutional stages that advanced economies underwent in the nineteenth and early twentieth centuries. This, as we will see, also has important implications for the institutional and technological trajectories of these emerging economic powers.

Trend 8 Century of Peace, Century of War

The twentieth century started off badly and continued to worsen on one very important aspect for our economic, social, and political lives: major wars and the senseless waste of millions of innocent lives. The two deadliest conflicts of human history were waged within the first fifty years of the twentieth century. But here is the surprising thing: the subsequent sixty

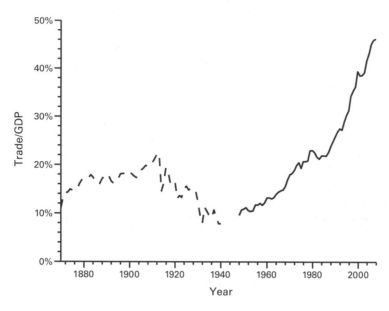

Figure 1.7
International trade, 1872–2008

years, even if not free of deadly civil and international wars, have been the
most peaceful throughout our recorded history. Figure 1.8 illustrates this
by showing both the total number of deaths from international wars per
100,000 and the twenty-one-year moving average of these numbers, which
makes the trends—the highs due to the two world wars and the lows over
the past sixty years—easier to see. Figure 1.9 shows the raw numbers and
the moving average for deaths from civil wars. Although there is a spike
following the end of colonial rule in much of the world, the trend toward
the past half-century has been toward fewer and less deadly civil wars.[10]
Figure 1.10, which focuses on the developed world, shows that the picture
as far as homicides are concerned is more complex. In the 1960s there was
a sharp increase in homicides in the United States, Canada, Australia, New
Zealand, and almost every European nation. Nevertheless, there has been
a sharp downward trend from 1990 onward.[11] Overall, the numbers taken
together suggest that though many parts of the world are still mired in violence and murder, many civil wars are still raging, and many governments
are still murdering their citizens with impunity, there is less violence in
most spheres of our lives today than 100 years ago.[12]

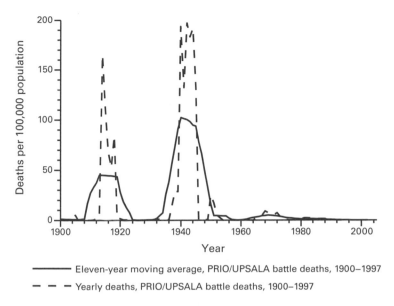

Figure 1.8
International battle deaths, 1900–1997

Trend 9   Counter-Enlightenment in Politics

Few would have predicted the rights revolution. But those who might have, like Denis Diderot or D'Holbach, would have put it as a corollary of the universal spread of the ideas and ideals of the Enlightenment, based on rational thought and empirical assessment. In contrast, these 100 years have also witnessed strong and often violent counter-Enlightenment movements playing a defining role in politics. The first half of the twentieth century was dominated by two such movements, fascism and communism, that rose to power in several countries, wreaking havoc and murdering millions. Fascism, and its more malignant cousin, Nazism, were stamped out after World War II, and their noxious remnants withered away as fascistic regimes in Greece, Portugal, Spain, and Latin America also left the stage.

The previous four decades, however, have witnessed another counter-Enlightenment movement: the increasing role of religion in politics. Although this trend cuts across religions, as illustrated by fundamentalist Christians becoming a force to be reckoned with in U.S. politics during the past half-century and ultra-Orthodox Judaism playing a more important role in Israeli and Middle Eastern politics, it is most dramatically illustrated

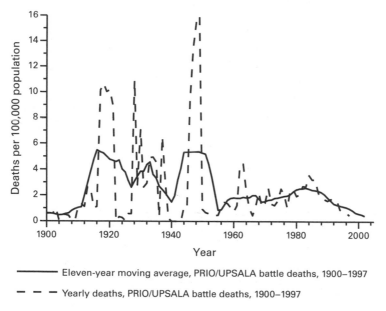

Figure 1.9
Civil war deaths, 1900–1997

by the resurgence of political Islam in the Middle East, North Africa, and South Asia. Following the more secular regimes that had sprung up in much of the region in the first sixty years or so of the twentieth century, there has been an increase in the role that religion plays in society and politics throughout the Muslim world, and this has prompted many to see an upcoming clash of civilizations, a view inevitably strengthened by the war on terror declared by President George W. Bush.

Trend 10   The Population Explosion, Resources, and the Environment

There are many more of us on planet Earth today than 100 years ago. Figure 1.11 plots the evolution of population over the past 100 years (and projections for the next 100 years for future reference).[13] It shows that population has increased from 1.5 billion in 1900 to 6.9 billion in 2010. Most of this increase has been in the relatively less prosperous parts of the world. The population of western Europe, North America, Australia, and New Zealand increased by only a factor of 1.7 during the same period. Together with increasing population and rising income per capita has come increasing

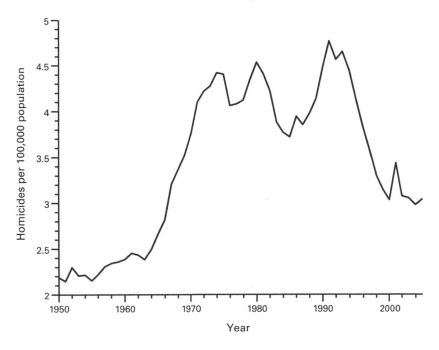

Figure 1.10
Homicide rates, 1950–2005

demand from and pressures on our environment. Many were worried about whether we would outgrow the ability of our planet to support us. The optimistic and pessimistic views on this were characterized by the famous wager between environmentalist Paul Ehrlich and economist Julian Simon about the prices of a bundle of scarce commodities. Ehrlich had predicted a demographic catastrophe and widespread scarcities because of rapid population growth. Challenged by Simon, he picked chromium, copper, nickel, tin, and tungsten as the five commodities that would experience increases in their inflation-adjusted prices between 1980 and 1990. The wager ended with a victory for the optimistic view when the inflation-adjusted prices of all five commodities fell. The victory may have been premature, however; since then, resource prices have been increasing as Figure 1.12, which plots the average prices of this bundle, shows. But resource prices are likely to be just a sideshow.[14] The more fundamental impact we have on our environment is from our prodigious fossil fuel consumption and increasing levels of carbon dioxide in the atmosphere, which will continue apace even if some resources, including oil, become scarce.

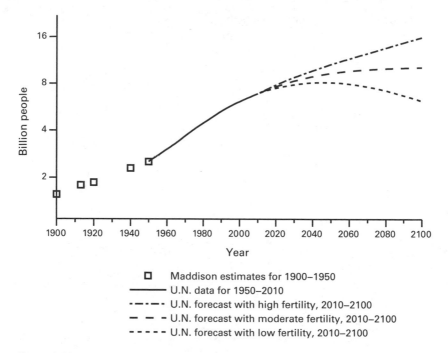

Figure 1.11
World population, 1900–2100

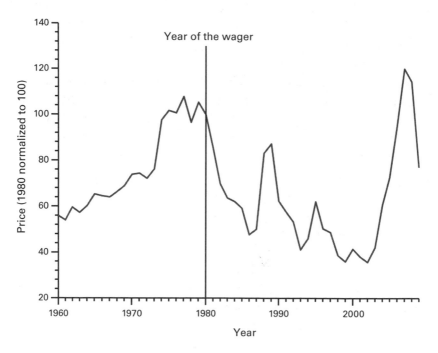

Figure 1.12
Price of commodities in the Ehrlich and Simon's wager, 1960–2009

**

These trends are clearly not independent. Understanding how they inter-relate is an important step in assessing how they will continue. The rela-tionships among these trends are undoubtedly multifaceted, and offering a unified explanation for such diverse trends would be foolhardy at best. But I would not be able to say much if I did not have a sort of framework enabling me to think, at least loosely, about why these trends shaped our century.

The framework I use to interpret these trends borrows heavily from my work with James A. Robinson.[15] At its center is the idea that technological change is at the root of economic growth, which accords well with the tech-nological nature of many of the trends I have identified. But I also maintain that it is institutions that shape the nature, pace, and spread of technologi-cal change. In this, I depart from what may be the de facto conventional wisdom in much of social science—the view that the strong causal link is from technologies to institutions and not the other way around, as I am arguing. A particular example of this view is the modernization theory, formulated by, among others, Martin Seymour Lipset, which sees a strong causal link from prosperity to democracy and political rights. Unfortu-nately, there is little support for the modernization theory in the data. For example, countries that have grown more rapidly since World War II or since the beginning of the twentieth century are no more likely to become more democratic than those growing more slowly.[16] I instead argue that institutional developments associated with, caused by, and causing the rights revolution are the main drivers of the technological and economic changes we have experienced over the past century.

Technological progress takes place and spreads most naturally under a specific type of economic institution, which we have called *inclusive*: institutions that provide incentives and opportunities for innovation and economic activity for a broad cross-section of society. These incentives are based on secure property rights for innovators, businesses, and workers, and opportunities are undergirded by a level playing field, lack of entry barriers into businesses and occupations, and basic public services and infrastruc-ture to enable participation in economic activity for a large cross-section of society. Inclusive economic institutions are supported by inclusive political institutions, which are defined by two characteristics: first, a pluralistic, broad-based distribution of political power, so that no single individual or group can exercise power and rule without constraints and in an arbitrary fashion; and second, sufficient state centralization, so that there is a sort of monopoly on violence in the hands of the state—rather than warlords, strongmen, or bandits—on which order and security over the territories making up a nation can be grounded.

At the other extreme from inclusive institutions are *extractive institutions*. Extractive economic institutions are characterized by insecure property rights for the majority, coercion, and lack of freedom directed at extracting resources from the majority for the benefit of a narrow elite, a playing field tilted to favor the elite, often thanks to entry barriers into businesses and occupations meant to create monopoly rents for them, and a general lack of opportunities and public services for most. These economic institutions are kept in place by extractive political institutions, concentrating power in the hands of a narrow group or interest without any meaningful checks or constraints on the exercise of this power. Another form of extractive political institutions emerges from lack of state centralization, making lawlessness and insecurity endemic (even if this is not always associated with the existence of a well-defined elite).

Technological change, and hence growth, is much more likely to take place under inclusive institutions because they provide opportunities and incentives to a large segment of the population. In fact, extractive institutions often explicitly block technological change and innovation because they are deemed to be destabilizing for the regime or against the interests of the narrow elite controlling power. Even though they do not foster an environment conducive to economic growth, extractive institutions have been the norm throughout history because they benefit those at the helm. The elite can enrich and avail themselves of the benefits of monopolizing political power, even if this comes at the cost of impoverishing and oppressing the rest of society. They will also be steadfastly opposed to many reforms because, just like technological change, reforms often erode the basis of their monopoly of power. Though the control of the elite can explain the emergence and persistence of extractive institutions, it is not the only significant factor ensuring their durability. Extractive institutions, just like other forms of organizations, have a social basis. They create a whole hierarchy of social organizations, with their own socialization and internalized norms. For extractive institutions, these are often based on various forms of authoritarian ideas and rigid hierarchies—not only in national politics but within villages, neighborhoods, families, and firms. So even within communities or families that bear the brunt of the poverty and repression wrought by extractive institutions, there will be individuals who will oppose change toward more inclusive institutions because their position within the social hierarchy will be disrupted and because they have been socialized within these institutions and internalized their values and norms.

But the world under extractive institutions is not a static one. Because extractive institutions involve the enrichment of a small group at the expense of the rest, the rest will sometimes rise up. The logic of extractive institutions, coming both from the monopolization of economic and political power in the hands of the elite and from the social basis of these institutions within every level of the social hierarchy, militates against change. All the same, the inherent conflict in society sometimes makes a dent in the fabric of extractive institutions, opening the way to more inclusive ones. This we have witnessed most recently with the Arab Spring, and with such landmark events as the Glorious Revolution of 1688–1689 in England and the French Revolution of 1789.

It is in this light that the first trend, the rights revolution, should be assessed. Though moves away from extractive toward inclusive institutions took place for centuries, ours has been the period in which such moves gathered speed and force. It is important that this revolution was not just one of change in political regimes, constitutions, and laws on parchment paper. Where inclusive institutions have taken hold most strongly, civil and political rights for most groups have also been expanded, and there has been a broad emancipation of individuals from the authoritarian social norms of communities and families that have acted as a microcosm of the more macroextractive institutions. In fact, inclusive institutions are not durable if they are superimposed on the social hierarchy and the socialization created by extractive institutions. Hence, though one can imagine a democracy in which individual liberties are not fully respected, that can never be a lasting inclusive regime. This is not to suggest that all revolutions or movements vying for more extensive rights inevitably lead to more inclusive institutions. Many such movements have led to changes in government, but without altering the underlying institutions or expanding the rights of the majority of the population, and some, best exemplified by the Bolshevik Revolution of 1917, have replaced one tyranny by a more murderous one. Even when the ultimate trajectory has been toward inclusive institutions, the path may be arduous and may even involve needless bloodshed, as was the case with the French Revolution. Nevertheless, the overall trend in the twentieth century was toward more inclusive institutions, which went hand-in-hand with the rights revolution.

The next five trends—the sweep of technology, unrelenting growth, uneven growth, the transformation of work, and the health revolution— all emanate, more or less directly, from this rights revolution. The technological breakthroughs we have witnessed over the past century could not have been possible in a world dominated by extractive institutions. The incentives, freedom, opportunities, and level playing field provided by the inclusive institutions taking hold in many parts of the world were the foundations of these technological changes in the same way that the proto-inclusive institutions that followed the Glorious Revolution in England were the fountainhead of the Industrial Revolution. Economic growth then followed directly from these technological breakthroughs. That this growth has been uneven is largely a consequence of the fact that inclusive institutions have spread unevenly in both the nineteenth and twentieth centuries. As nations that adopted relatively inclusive institutions prospered by investing in developing their own technologies and often adopting the best technologies from other leading economies, those with extractive institutions often created few incentives for their citizens to undertake such investments or use these technologies, and often they actively blocked industrialization and the use of modern technologies they deemed destabilizing to their regimes.[17] The fifth and sixth trends, the transformation of work and the health revolution, also followed from the same forces. The former did so essentially directly from the nature of the technological changes of our century. The latter, fueled by better drugs and vaccines, is also one of the most noteworthy fruits of our greater technological ingenuity. But another aspect of inclusive institutions that had taken root by the middle of the twentieth century also played a major role in the health revolution. The more significant changes in health and life expectancy, as figure 1.6 shows, came in developing countries, many of which were still under extractive regimes not only bent on defending the privileges of a few, but also without the capacity to deliver health care or even drugs and vaccines to their population even if they had any inclination to do so. But the impetus for such actions came from the richer countries and their international organizations, such as the World Health Organization. This we also owe mostly to the rights revolution. It became accepted that not only individuals, women, and minorities should be given rights and protected at home, but help should also be given to those suffering around the world, making the health revolution a uniquely illustrative consequence of several immediate forces unleashed by the rights revolution.

The seventh trend, technology without borders, also clearly technological in nature, is another consequence of the rights revolution. But to understand its full import, we need to take a small digression. Though inclusive
institutions are the mainspring of technological change, this is not to say
that growth is impossible under extractive institutions. All else equal, those
in command of extractive institutions would also like to achieve as much
economic growth as possible because they would be the beneficiaries of this
growth. The problem arises when growth necessitates new technologies
that will strip their rents or destabilize their power. But economic growth
can take off even under extractive institutions when it can proceed without
endangering the stability of these regimes and relying on businesses controlled by the state, the elite, or their allies. Two scenarios make this sort of
growth under extractive institutions possible. The first is when the comparative advantage of a society is in a well-defined sector that can still function
fairly effectively even if it is under the control of a small group of people in
society. The exemplars are the Caribbean colonies, such as Barbados, Cuba,
and Haiti, between the sixteenth and eighteenth centuries, which generated rapid growth despite harshly extractive institutions based on slavery
and sugar plantations, controlled by a small planter class. The second is
when growth can be driven by a process of catch-up and technology transfer from a more advanced set of countries.[18] The rapid growth of Soviet Russia, a quintessential example of extractive institutions, was underpinned by
this type of catch-up between the 1930s and the early 1970s, set in motion
in part by the forceful, ruthless transfer of resources out of agriculture into
industry. In both of these scenarios, though it can take place rapidly and
for an extended period of time, growth under extractive institutions is
ultimately limited. The plantation colonies stagnated and declined when
the world demand for sugar declined. Soviet Russia stagnated and declined
when the limits of forceful industrialization were reached. None of these
societies generated much technological progress.

The growth of China today is another example of growth under extractive institutions, but with a major difference. The onset of technology without borders has meant that the extent and pace of growth under extractive
institutions are much greater today. Germany and Russia went through a
process of catch-up in the nineteenth century. Though they reached higher
growth rates than the leading economies of the time, the United States
and the United Kingdom, this was for a limited period of time, and it was
made possible in both Germany and Russia by deeply rooted changes in

the structure of society—changes that ultimately destabilized and felled the regimes in place in these nations. China has been able to achieve rapid catch-up growth for over three decades, with much more limited threats to its extractive institutions, partly because the nature of technology has changed. Catch-up growth for Germany and Russia at the end of the nineteenth century and for Japan and South Korea in the second half of the twentieth century involved developing industries, building a domestic market, and undergoing a process of structural, social, and institutional changes. Even if they benefited from catch-up growth, particularly because they did not have to invent all of the necessary technology anew, they could not simply import technology to produce for the world market some of the component tasks in textiles, transport, chemistry, or metallurgy. In contrast, recent changes in the nature of technology and the globalization of production have meant that instead of having to develop an entire industry, an emerging market economy can house just some of the tasks, such as assembly and operation. This has not only enabled China to grow very rapidly by relying on world technology and leveraging its cheap and abundant labor force, but has also mollified the demands for structural, social, and institutional changes that previous societies undergoing catch-up growth experienced. Here we encounter a paradoxical consequence of the technological breakthroughs originating from inclusive institutions: to possibly extend the likelihood of one type of extractive institutions in another part of the world.

In fact, the paradox might be deeper. If Chinese growth, with reduced demand for societal change, is one side of these technological break-throughs and offshoring opportunities, then the fifth trend, the transformation of work and wages, together with the inequality gap that has opened up within advanced economies as illustrated in figures 1.4 and 1.5, may be the other. Put differently, the globalization of production that the technology without borders has created may have fueled rapid Chinese growth and retarded its institutional changes.

Extractive institutions are not forever. Neither are inclusive institutions. They are constantly threatened by groups that want to expand their political power at the expense of the rest and use their power to gain economic privileges, and then use those economic privileges as leverage to gain more political power. When such a process goes on unchecked, it can bring down inclusive institutions. The sharp increases in inequality in the United States and elsewhere in the advanced world, which partly flow from the same technological and globalization developments that are fueling Chinese growth, may be doubly ominous here. First, the rise in inequality has created a class of very wealthy citizens who can use their wealth to gain more political power—partly to defend their wealth and partly to further their economic, political, and ideological agendas. Second, as also shown in figures 1.4 and 1.5, it has thinned the middle classes, which have often been a strong supporter of inclusive institutions.

The outlines of the framework I have offered so far also make clear why the second part of the eighth trend, the decline of war and violence, is also a consequence of the rights revolution. This is partly for the same reasons that the rights revolution led to greater freedoms of individuals and increased protection of the rights of women and minorities. It also discourages war for several reasons. First, these freedoms and rights are naturally in conflict with murderous wars and violent militaristic adventures. Second, as Jack Snyder has argued, many wars have their origins in domestic political conflicts, which are much more likely under extractive institutions, and the spread of the rights revolution should make this less likely also.[19] Third, the rights revolution is also the philosophical foundation of the changes in international organizations and norms that have been acting, albeit imperfectly, as a restraint on international war. European warring declined, for example, following the Congress of Vienna in 1815 because there were more clearly laid expectations and more communication among states and less tolerance for unilateral militaristic actions. The United Nations has played the same role since World War II. The more recent Libyan experience demonstrates that even domestic atrocities create risks of foreign intervention, putting further restraints on civil wars and the murderous tendencies of authoritarian regimes.

But there is more to it. A lasting transition from extractive to inclusive institutions also necessitates a fundamental change in the social basis of these institutions—in particular, a move away from the authoritarian and hierarchical structure of families and communities. I believe that it is this transformation, underway in many parts of the world, that is in large part responsible for the decline of war and violence. In the U.S. context, some, like conservative commentator Charles Murray, have claimed that it is the collapse of parental authority over youngsters that led to the increase in inner-city violence in the 1970s and 1980s, but the more remarkable trend is for the secular decline in violence that has gone hand-in-hand with the decline of the authoritarian community and family structures.[20] It is also reasonable to conjecture, though this is highly speculative to say the least, that by reducing the importance of agriculture and other manual tasks, the transformation of work may also accelerate the decline of the social structures and norms supporting extractive institutions. This is because authoritarian, hierarchical community structures and authoritarian, patriarchal families built partly on the threat of violence are more likely to prevail when work is based on physical labor.

But then what explains the explosion of war in the first half of the twentieth century and the counter-Enlightenment trends of both the first and the second halves? The honest answer is that I do not know. But the framework I have outlined gives some clues. The rights revolution, by going against the social fabric of a society largely developed under extractive institutions, may have also sown the seeds of a strong backlash. This, combined with intense distributional conflicts that have been ongoing in the wake of the collapse of these extractive regimes, may have created the platform for these counter-Enlightenment movements. This perspective becomes a little more plausible when we consider that communism, fascism, and religious extremism in politics have all emerged in the midst of conflict about the distribution of income and resources in society and mobilized those discontented and alienated by the changes around them. I discuss these issues in a little more detail below in the context of other causes of the rise of political Islam.

Finally, the tenth trend—the explosion of population and the greater strains we are putting on our environment—is another paradoxical consequence of the worldwide development of inclusive institutions and the technological changes that flowed from them. These technological changes have enabled much more rapid growth in output around the world. As we have seen, they have also generated much better medical technologies, drugs, and vaccines, preventing the premature deaths of millions. This has meant that many women who would have died early now survive to childbearing age, and in societies that have not yet undergone the fertility transition, it has translated into a population explosion. This much greater population does not by itself pose a major problem for our planet so long as other economic and social challenges are met. But together with the rise in income per capita, it has have also been associated with a massive increase in our fossil fuel emissions, which now threaten the stability of our climate.

***

Now, armed with a list of trends that have defined our epoch and a (preliminary) framework that enables us to link them and think about them, I move on to discuss whether we may expect to see the continuation or reversal of these trends and how these developments might shape the planet we will bequeath to our grandchildren.

Prediction 1   The Rights Revolution Continued?

The predictions of the modernization theory and Francis Fukuyama's declaration, based on a similar reasoning, of the "end of history" and the triumph of democratic capitalism notwithstanding, not only is the rights revolution quite incomplete, but our prosperity is no guarantee for its maintenance and expansion. There are in fact several roadblocks, mostly by-products of the other major trends discussed here, on the way to further expansion of political and civil rights. Most important among these are:

• Democratic and inclusive institutions and, by implication, civil and political rights in the United States, one of the most prosperous and most democratic countries of the twentieth century, are under attack. These are coming from two distinct quarters. The first is a direct threat to American democracy. As I noted, U.S. income inequality and society have polarized, creating a class of very wealthy Americans who are increasingly playing a defining role in politics. Perhaps in response to this, money—as a source of campaign contributions and through lobbying and other influence activities—has become even more essential in politics over the past several decades. This all bodes ill for the health of American democracy, and if American democracy falters, so will political and civil rights at home and abroad. The second is a direct attack on individual and minority liberties emanating from the so-called war on terror, started under President George W. Bush and continued vigorously under President Barack Obama, which can spill over to corrode American democracy.

• Chinese growth, particularly compared to the economic problems of the past several years in the United States and Europe, creates the illusion of an alternative, authoritarian path to riches. Democracy is a burden and a hindrance, the argument goes, and enlightened authoritarianism can better serve the people. Perhaps it should be no surprise that this authoritarian path is enthralling to aspiring autocrats in Asia and Africa. There is some enthusiasm for it even in the United States and Europe. Although this is a faulty reading of the causes and nature of Chinese growth, it does not imply that a turn toward authoritarianism in some of these countries can be ruled out-of-hand.

These threats notwithstanding, the odds are in favor of the rights revolution to continue, albeit at a relatively slow pace, and for reasons very different from those advanced by the modernization theory. The optimistic case that the rights revolution can overcome these roadblocks is based on four factors. First, inclusive institutions, though by no means irreversible, have a resilience of their own and have been able to overcome comparable challenges, although, for example, they proved to be just strong enough during the Gilded Age to stand up to the robber barons who were as wealthy as, and even more ruthless than, their counterparts today. In western Europe, inclusive institutions have followed a somewhat different trajectory, and even if they are facing challenges related to the future of the European Union and the euro, the diversity of inclusive institutions across advanced economies is a strong guarantee against their wholesale takeover by some narrow band of moneyed interests. Second, the spread of the Internet and social media has added another pillar to the support of inclusive institutions. We have recently witnessed the strength of this pillar in how Wikipedia, Google, Reddit, and several other prominent sites have stopped antipiracy laws that would have seriously curtailed free speech and exchange on the Internet. Third, and somewhat more speculative, the transformation of work and the already significant impact of the rights revolution on social structure may have dented the authoritarian community and family structures, in the process weakening future support for encroachment on individual and minority rights and liberties. Finally, the framework I have outlined also suggests that the double-digit Chinese growth rates, even if they benefit from the globalization of technology and production, are ultimately transitory, and unless China fundamentally reforms its institutions in an inclusive direction, its economy will run out of steam, probably within the next two or three decades as China reaches income per capita levels around 30 to 40 percent of that of the United States. This is bad news for the welfare of the citizens of the world's most populous country. In fact, rather than institutional reforms, the slowdown of growth in China may even bring out the Communist Party's more authoritarian and repressive bent. But it also implies that the lure of the authoritarian growth models is likely to fade.

The pessimistic case, that even if the rights revolution is not reversed, its advance will be slow, is based on the endurance of extractive institutions that still surround us. In fact, many of the societies under extractive institutions today are different from China because their main challenge is not in creating more broadly based participation in politics and ensuring pluralism. Rather, many of these societies still lack political centralization; thus, their path to inclusive institutions will be more arduous as it will have to involve first the building of state institutions and subsequently guarantees that these institutions are not captured by some narrow interests. The experiences in Afghanistan, Haiti, and Somalia, to name three notable cases that have received attention recently, highlight the difficulties in this process.

So overall, we can be cautiously optimistic that the rights revolution will continue and spread, even if slowly and imperfectly. I also argue that this revolution will probably have a defining effect on the direction of the other major trends. All the same, optimism should not lead to complacency. One of the major differences between the framework I have tried to articulate and the modernization theory is that there is nothing inevitable about the continuation of the rights revolution, and it will only be actions by millions of individuals around the world that will defend and advance this revolution and the inclusive institutions built around it.

Prediction 2   The Future of Technology

Much can be written about the future of technology: about which functions can be effectively performed by robots; the reach of new health technologies and drugs; whether cars, trucks, and aircraft can fully dispense with their drivers and pilots; whether robots can clean our houses and mow our lawns; how we can better use the abundance of information around us; and so on. But without going into these details, the macropicture is clear: there is little evidence that we are running out of innovations. This is not only because there are literally millions of ideas that can be recombined into new ones to generate new processes and products, but also because every innovation poses new problems and opens the way for yet more innovations, as illustrated most recently by smart phones, tablets, and social media, which have created new industries centered on developing applications for these platforms. Another factor boding well for the

future of technology is the ability of our society to direct technological
change to sectors, products, and factors of production that will most benefit from improvements.[21] Recent work by Walker Hanlon illustrates one
example of this type of directed technological change using evidence from
nineteenth-century innovations. He shows how Civil War era disruption
of U.S. cotton supplies to the British industry led to rapid improvements
in textile processes using Indian cotton.[22] A more contemporary example
comes from the response of the U.S. pharmaceutical industry to changes
in the market size for different types of drugs driven by the baby boom
and the subsequent baby bust. The evidence suggests that there were significantly more new drugs and new molecular entities for diseases whose
market expanded.[23]

The main threat to our technological vibrancy comes not from an imminent drying up of new ideas but from a wholesale shift away from inclusive
institutions. In the absence of this, innovations and technological ingenuity
are set to go on, and even if those threats to our inclusive institutions should
not be underestimated, we are not in imminent danger of the whole edifice
that has developed over the past century collapsing in front of our very eyes.

Prediction 3   Will Growth Relent?

Economic growth, sustained economic growth for that matter, is not a law
of nature. It can slow down or even halt. But there are several reasons to
think that we are not near the end of the process of economic growth.
First, there are no obvious reasons to expect a slowdown in technological
change, the main engine of economic growth. Second, there is rapid catch-
up growth not only in China but throughout the rest of the developing
world. This is not to suggest that there are no dangers to watch out for.
Advanced economies, in particular the United States and western Europe,
are struggling with their own fiscal and economic problems, and though
these problems are mostly short term and much more superficial than they
appear, the possibility of policy mistakes creating more profound problems
cannot be entirely ruled out. There is also a limit to how much we can count
on developing nations to spearhead world growth because their growth
relies on demand from advanced economies and the continued globalization of technology and production (and is thus dependent on the economic
health of the United States and western Europe), and because some of this
growth will likely slow as the low-hanging catch-up fruits are exhausted.

All in all, absent a major move away from inclusive institutions at the world level, our grandchildren should also be writing about how unrelenting growth has been in their past century.

Prediction 4   How Uneven Will Growth Be?

It would be utopian to hope that economic growth in the next century will ensure convergence between rich and poor nations. But there are reasons to expect that it will not be as uneven as twentieth-century growth. This is for several reasons. First, the rights revolution, together with its more inclusive institutions, is likely to spread to more countries during the next century, albeit slowly and imperfectly. Second, the globalization of technology and production is likely to continue, creating greater demand for cheap labor all around the world, even if it is located in countries still ruled by largely extractive institutions. Third, we may also expect some changes in the nature of extractive institutions, in particular, as many civil war–torn areas in sub-Saharan Africa and Asia start that process of state centralization and state building. In most cases, this process will be under the auspices of authoritarian governments, which, though often quite predatory, still create an environment where there is some law and order—in particular, favoring themselves and the elite surrounding them. This then allows more effective exploitation of natural resources for which world demand has been increasing, and can attract foreign investment to take advantage of cheap labor.

Prediction 5   The Transformation of Work Continued

The trend of technology and machines replacing manual labor and various routine tasks is set to continue for several more decades. This, combined with increasing levels of income, which tend to change the composition of demand, means the continuation of the structural transformation in many nations. Employment in agriculture will be less important, and services will be more important throughout sub-Saharan Africa, Asia, and Latin America. In advanced economies, the erosion of various middle-skill occupations is also likely to continue. But there should be no presumption that either of these two trends will inexorably lead to greater income inequality. The transition from agriculture to manufacturing and services can often act as an equalizing force, in particular lifting millions from poverty—even if the conditions in urban areas and nonagricultural sectors awaiting most migrants are still harsh and opportunities limited.

Although technological changes and the associated transformation of work in advanced economies, particularly in the United States, have contributed to worsening income inequality over the past three decades, and though the possibility that future advances in cheap robotics sharply reducing the demand for low- and middle-skill labor cannot be ruled out, this consequence is not inevitable either. First, U.S. inequality rose not only because of technology but also because the increase in the supply of education slowed down and due to institutional and policy changes favoring the top of the distribution. The United States should thus be able to create new middle-class jobs by investing in high-quality precollege education (both K–12 and prekindergarten), even if these would not be the sort of manual, middle-skill, middle-class jobs that our parents' generation had access to. Second, technological change has not just reduced the demand for all types of labor except those of engineers and managers; it has at the same time increased the demand for, and employment in, a variety of service occupations such as health technology, food preparation, and personal care. We may expect many of these occupations to command higher wages in the next several decades because technology will probably continue to favor them; because the demand for these services and the workers performing them is likely to expand as a result of the rise in incomes; and because, seeing these trends, workers are likely to invest in skills useful in such occupations and increase their earnings. Third, the directed nature of technology may play an important role. The path of change of technology is pliable and will respond to profit incentives and policy. If employment in service occupations expands, we may also expect technological developments directed at improving productivity in these tasks, which may also contribute to the emergence of a new middle class. Finally, whether there is a new middle class will also be a function of tax and labor market policies; a more progressive tax code can limit further polarization in the earnings and income distributions.

Put differently, how the gains from growth within a nation are shared is not determined just by the path of technology, but also by institutions and political choices of that nation. These will not only affect the supply of skills available to work with different types of technologies and the distribution of resources within society but also the evolution of technology.

Prediction 6   The Health Revolution Continued

There should be little doubt that the health revolution will continue. Not only will our children and grandchildren in advanced nations live healthier and longer lives than we are, their cousins in the poorer parts of the world will also be much healthier than their parents and grandparents. This is again mostly because of better technology, better drugs, and better vaccines being developed and spreading more rapidly across the world. It will also be helped with greater awareness about what sorts of infrastructural investments have to be made for public health. Of course, there will be hiccups on the way, especially because of all-too-avoidable famines in East Africa still failing to be avoided. The delivery of public health services will probably be slower than we might wish. But barring major wars, the trend toward convergence and health will continue. What this implies for economic growth is more debatable. The view from the World Health Organization and some economists such as Jeff Sachs is that there will be a huge growth dividend from improvements in health. But similar developments since the 1950s do not seem to have led to major growth dividends, even as they have improved lives and welfare around the world massively.[24] Thus, the most likely scenario is that the continuation of the health revolution will also create much better and healthier lives, but will not by itself be a major driver of economic growth.

As with all other trends toward improved lives and conditions, the biggest threat to the health revolution comes from a reversal in the rights revolution. First, there will be a limit to how health care delivery can be improved further unless there are some institutional improvements in many parts of sub-Saharan Africa and Asia. Second, a reversal in the rights revolution—or its conception—in the advanced nations may make them turn away from the investments and the foreign aid necessary to improve health around the world. To the extent that such reversals are unlikely, the continuation of the health revolution should be secure.

Prediction 7   The Future of Globalization

Though fueled by the technological breakthroughs in communication and transport, globalization has also been a choice. Figure 1.7 shows how an earlier episode of globalization came to an end amid turmoil and war. This is a possibility for our current wave as well, even if it is less likely because in many ways, the world has become even more integrated and reversing it just by changing trade policies will be less easy. In fact, new advances will likely increase the globalization of technology, facilitating offshoring and outsourcing of tasks that previously required person-to-person contact, such as consulting advice or medical diagnosis.

There are two reasons, however, to think that the pace of globalization of technology will be slower than before. First, the main impetus for this change, wages in labor-abundant, low-wage countries such as China, India, and Indonesia, have already started increasing as a result of the very process of globalization exploiting these differences. Second, Chinese growth may come to a screeching end, and with it, part of the system of the international division of labor may start faltering.

Prediction 8   The Peaceful Century?

If the twentieth was the century of war and century of peace, will the twenty-first be just the century of peace? There are reasons to think that the answer is yes, but there is room for concern as well. On the positive side, we have seen that both international and civil wars have been declining over the past sixty years, and despite some very deadly civil conflicts, such as the ones in Rwanda and the Balkans, recent decades have been more peaceful than past ones. Moreover, as figure 1.10 illustrates, in the more developed parts of the world, other forms of violence have also been in decline. The root causes of these trends, the rights revolution and its ramifications including changes in attitudes and norms, and the development of international institutions protecting world peace are likely to continue. For example, as the rights revolution spreads to other parts of the world, the hope is that there will be fewer wars resulting from domestic political calculations, and the values and social norms consistent with the rights revolution should make violence of all sorts less popular and less likely in much of the world. Other trends in institutions might also help. A first step toward inclusive institutions in many parts of the world will be further state centralization. A direct consequence of the transfer of the capacity of violence from its many sources to the state in places such as Somalia, the Congo, Afghanistan, and many parts of Pakistan will also be a reduction in various types of violence and murder.

One specific threat going in the opposite direction needs to be mentioned. The international order and organizations such as the United Nations that have played an important role in reducing war during the past sixty years have been designed for specific problems, for example, wars between the United States and the Soviet Union. The challenges ahead, however, will be very different, for instance, potential conflict between China and its neighbors. So it remains an open question whether these institutions will be up to the task of dealing with such emerging conflicts.

Prediction 9   From Counter-Enlightenment to Enlightenment?

Though fascism is now a distant memory, the defining role of religion in the politics of many regions is a clear and present reality. Is this something that will also decline like violence, as tolerance and rational thought replace extremism? There is no easy answer to this question, in part because our understanding of the causes of the increasing importance of religion in politics is still quite incomplete. My best guess at the moment is that the increasing role that Islam has been playing in politics in the Middle East, North Africa, and parts of South Asia is a result of three intersecting trends. The first is that it is part of the counter-Enlightenment—the reaction of the values and attitudes of individuals brought up with an authoritarian and traditional communities and families to bewildering, threatening changes around them. An illustrative example comes from Sayyid Qutb (1906–1966). Qutb was an Egyptian intellectual, theorist, author of several books, and leading member of the Egyptian Muslim Brotherhood in the 1950s and 1960s. He was one of the inspirations of many different shades of political Islam, including al Qaeda. Qutb's radicalization, during his studies in the United States, was in part a response to what he saw as modernity characterized by materialism, sexual promiscuity, and a lack of spirituality, engulfing not only America but also spreading to his home nation, Egypt. The second is that the process of modernization in many Muslim nations has taken place under extractive institutions, leaving large segments of society behind. So the support for political Islam often has a distributional element, standing up more for the less well-to-do and the disenfranchised (Saudi Arabia notwithstanding). The evidence from the attitudes of political parties built on some Islamist principles, such as the Justice and Development Party in Turkey, the Muslim Brotherhood in Egypt, and Ennahda in Tunisia, suggests that though they are as likely to work to serve their interests by hook or crook, they also speak more for this segment of the population than the regimes they are challenging. This is highlighted by recent research by Erik Meyersson, who looks at the implications of the Islamist party narrowly winning power in some Turkish municipalities in 1994.[25] He finds that in places where there were such narrow victories and local control shifted to members of this Islamist party, girls were actually significantly more—not less—likely to go to school, probably because conservative parents felt more secure about sending their daughters to school and perhaps also because this party cared more about the schooling of the less well-to-do than had the elite secular parties that had dominated Turkish politics until then. The third factor potentially contributing to the increasing role of Islam is a widespread feeling in many of these countries that the West has been imperialistic and has played an instrumental role in the relative underdevelopment of the region, a feeling strengthened by the recent rhetoric of the "clash of civilizations."

We should then expect that the rights revolution will be particularly slow in taking root in many of these countries because all three trends still shape domestic politics and views in the region and also because many versions of political Islam are opposed to several aspects of the rights revolution, including certain rights and freedoms of individuals, women, and minorities. Nevertheless, I believe that the rights revolution is likely to spread to this part of the world too. This is again not because of the factors emphasized by the modernization theory, but because of the political and social dynamics in the region. We have already seen with the Arab Spring that the extractive regimes in many countries in the region are less stable than they appeared just years ago, and political change is coming to the region, even if there will be many false starts and much continued conflict over it within the next several decades. Moreover, more moderate and popular versions of the religious political movements, such as the Muslim Brotherhood, are bringing more political and civil rights to a significant fraction of the population, and this should ultimately pave the way for a greater expansion in rights for everybody. Nevertheless, it would be naive to expect a wholesale embrace of Enlightenment in much of the region within the next several decades. More likely is a de facto expansion of political and civil rights to individuals, women, and minorities, even as the discourse within much of the society still remains influenced by religion.

In focusing on the role of religion in politics, I do not mean to rule out the possibility that there may be new counter-Enlightenment forces emerging in the next century. An obvious candidate is the resurgence of fascism or other forms of militarism in China or the United States or both. Sinclair Lewis declared in 1935 that "when fascism comes to America, it will be wrapped in the flag and carrying a cross," and perhaps the increasing role of religion in U.S. politics, the war on terror, and future conflicts with China make this more likely. Another candidate might be an antimodernist movement opposed to technology and economic progress, perhaps partly motivated by the valid concern to save our planet from climate change and other adverse environmental consequences—and paradoxically partly spawned by the rights revolution that makes people more concerned about the rights and welfare of others. Though possible, I think these threats are largely far-fetched.

Prediction 10   Population, Resources, and the Environment in the Twenty-First Century

The U.N. forecasts about world population, under low-, moderate-, and high-fertility scenarios, are shown in figure 1.11. Two important conclusions follow from this: first, population will continue to grow for quite a while, and second, it is likely to reach a plateau at some point in the next century. The world can easily accommodate this expanded population, and there is little reason to fear any acute resource scarcities or population-related disturbances. Even if Julian Simon would have lost the wager at today's prices as figure 1.12 shows, he was right in the big picture that technology will be quite adept at dealing with scarcities reflected in prices— for example, by channeling innovations to overcome bottlenecks, as my discussion of directed technological change illustrates. The more critical question relates to climate change and our fossil fuel consumption, partly because the damage that fossil fuel emissions create is a textbook case of the tragedy of the commons. Unless we introduce appropriate carbon taxes and other regulations, the damage each of us creates on the environment is not priced, and we will tend to continue to emit fossil fuels even as this threatens our planet. Figure 1.13 shows the evolution of carbon emissions, concentration of carbon in the atmosphere, and the date of the Kyoto Protocol.[26] Not only have we been increasing carbon emissions since the turn of the century but, in fact, given the rapid industrialization in China and many other emerging economies, there appears to be no feasible way of achieving a reduction anytime soon. Instead, we have pinned our hopes to two other precarious developments—one technological, the other political.

On the technological front, we need breakthroughs in alternative energy and the energy grid so as to find low-carbon ways of producing and delivering energy. We may rely on geoengineering solutions to reduce the impact of already emitted carbon and reduce current emissions through processes such as carbon capture. But these are stopgap measures. Ultimately the only way to ensure the survival of our planet is to transition to cleaner energy. This is a tall order, but perhaps not as much as it might first appear, thanks again to the directed nature of technological changes. In particular, to be viable, clean energy does not need to be fully cost-effective in the medium term. With the right policies, the switch to alternative energy can take place when these are up to 50 percent more expensive than fossil-fuel-based energy. Once they have a sufficient market share and are expected to expand, there will also be greater incentives for technology to

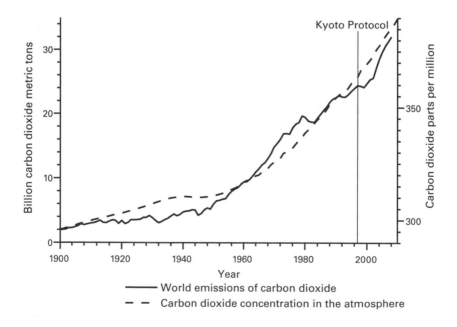

Figure 1.13
Global carbon dioxide emissions and concentration, 1900–2008

be endogenously directed toward these technologies and away from the older, dirtier technologies.[27] These innovations, together with the natural learning-by-doing that will take place with cleaner techniques, can take us toward our target. Although this scenario is on the whole optimistic, it has within it a major danger: the prospect of geoengineering, and technological advances in clean technology might work as a pretext for not taking action in reducing carbon emissions and switching to cleaner energy sources. If so, our belief in our technological mastery might ultimately create much more damage than good.

On the political front, we need an international agreement so that the transition to alternative energy sources takes place in a concerted manner even if this means higher costs in the short term for participating countries. Our track record so far does not inspire confidence. There is a case for being pessimistic here, but an important factor again pushes in the opposite direction: the rights revolution, if it does indeed continue to spread, will also tend to make people care more about the welfare of those who will suffer because of our unwillingness to take action against climate change. We are already seeing this in the willingness of a subset of the population in the developed world to make sacrifices, albeit small ones, to reduce their own carbon emissions or contribute in other ways to the preservation of the environment. If this trend continues and there is enough demand from electorates for an international accord to fight climate change, politicians will have to fall in line.

At the end, as with the other trends that have made and should continue to make our world a better place, our hopes for the healthy future of our planet must again be pinned on the continuation and strengthening of the rights revolution.

Acknowledgments

I thank David Autor, Tarek Hassan, Pascual Restrepo, Jim Robinson, and Alex Wolitzky for suggestions and comments.

2   Through the Darkness to a Brighter Future

Angus Deaton

The Threatening Sky

When Keynes wrote his famous essay, "Economic Possibilities for Our Grandchildren," times were tough and a dim future loomed. But Keynes warned his readers not to confuse the short run with the long run and reassured them that the long-term fundamentals were sound. The technical progress that had brought the world so far could be relied on to take it a great deal further. He worried that there were circumstances that could derail progress, and he made his predictions conditional on there being "no important wars and no important increases in population." World War II and the population explosion surely qualify as important, yet living standards today are as high as he predicted.

Today, too, times are tough. The United States is limping out of the Great Recession, the worst since Keynes's own time. The future of the European economy is far from guaranteed, and the possible collapse of the euro could precipitate long-term stagnation or worse. Growth in India and China is stalling. I write in the immediate aftermath of the devastation wrought by Hurricane Sandy in the northeastern United States. The steady rise of sea level all but guarantees that such hurricanes will grow more frequent, and while the repairs and (possibly futile) defensive expenditures will stimulate GDP, this is a classic case of GDP and human well-being moving in opposite directions.

Perhaps, like Keynes, we can predict that these short-run threats will dissipate under the relentless drive of human ingenuity to make life better. In the long run, we will all be dead. A hundred years from now, even my grandchildren will (almost certainly) be dead, but my grandchildren's grandchildren will perhaps be richer and healthier than we can imagine. Yet today, it is not just the immediate environment that threatens. The short-term problems look like symptoms of deeper processes that are not about to go away.

Population growth and world wars are perhaps not the threats today that they were for Keynes, but unregulated climate change is a new and enormous danger. The long-term prospects for climate control are poor; the 2012 presidential election in the United States was notable for its avoidance of the issue; and lower growth rates in India and China, even if moderating the growth of emissions, will also lower the priority that Indians and Chinese assign to tackling climate change.

The growth in living standards was threatened even before climate change. The growth of per capita GDP in the United States had been falling decade by decade even before the financial crisis. Even starting after the reconstruction spurt in Europe after World War II, European growth rates were falling long before the euro crisis. Perhaps the gods of technical change have abandoned us. Many writers have bemoaned that current technical progress is almost entirely information based, that other aspects of production and consumption have changed little in the last thirty years, and that the Internet, e-mail, smart phones, iPods, and tablets are no more than beguiling toys that add as little to human welfare as they add to productivity growth.

Many of us are also concerned that the grotesque expansions in inequality of the past thirty years will undermine economic growth. When growth is not widely shared and when a small fraction of the population grows fabulously wealthy, the power that the rich poses is a risk to the prosperity of everyone else. The superwealthy have little need for public goods, public health care, or public education, or even for some kinds of basic infrastructure. Yet education and health are part of welfare in and of themselves, and a broadly educated and healthy population is required to support the innovation on which growth depends. At the same time, the rich often have both the incentives and the means to block the creative destruction that is required at each new round of innovation.

Those who are doing well will organize to protect what they have, including in ways that benefit them at the expense of the majority—for example, by lobbying for special interest rules and regulations. Financial crises have happened throughout history, just as hurricanes have happened throughout history. But just as the latest hurricane is worse because it was fueled by rising sea levels and so is a portent of ever more frequent hurricanes, the latest financial crisis is worse if it was partly caused by an overly powerful and underregulated financial sector.

The United States spends 18 percent of its gross domestic product (GDP) on health care, much of it on procedures and devices that do little to improve health. Technical progress in health care is driven as much by what the government will pay for as by its payoff in extending life spans. And the bigger and richer the health care industry becomes, the more power it has to influence the payment rules and prevent the establishment of any authority that could check the cost effectiveness of new procedures. A system in which the government pays for most of health spending while lobbyists set the rules and prices is a system that allows the few to plunder the many. Overgrown financial and health care sectors are effective rent-seeking machines for their executives while they reduce the well-being of the rest of us. Such processes put a brake on economic growth, and their pervasiveness can justify pessimism about the prospects for long-run growth.

The long-established increase in life expectancy is also losing momentum. The reductions in infant and child mortality that propelled the first expansion in life spans have been replaced, over the past half-century, by reductions in mortality at higher ages. Reductions in cardiovascular mortality among the middle-aged and elderly have been driven by reductions in smoking, drug-based methods for controlling hypertension, and better treatments for those who have had heart attacks. Any reductions in mortality that once came from better nutrition have long been exhausted, and we are now going the other way as the increasing prevalence of obesity and diabetes acts to reverse the mortality decline.

Cancer is the other great killer, and the war on cancer, long declared, is far from won. And even if progress continues, future mortality declines must come—not among the young, among whom mortality is already very low, but among the elderly. While I (and other old people) am better off with a few more years to spend with my grandchildren, and even to speculate about the lives of my great-great-grandchildren a century from now, advances at the end of life merely postpone the inevitable for a few years and do little to advance life expectancy.

This is a gloomy picture, and it would not be hard to persuade oneself that there is little hope for further increases in living standards or life expectancy. Perhaps we can feel better about this if, unlike me, you can bring yourself to accept the argument that living standards are overrated in any case, that human well-being does not improve with economic growth, and that we should seek improvements in well-being elsewhere, through better social relationships, better health, and more leisure.

Even so, I remain cautiously optimistic.

As I have stated them, the negative arguments are too strong and, in some cases, wrong. They are also too narrow in both scope and content. Their scope includes only rich countries, ignoring what has been happening and might happen for most of the people on the planet. Even if my great-great-grandchildren may not be much richer or much longer lived than their grandparents, the prospects for Africans, Indians, and Chinese are brighter. Keynes's content was also too narrow. He talked about material living standards, not about health and life expectancy. But even health and wealth are far from exhausting the possibilities for improvement for our (and others') descendants.

The Brighter Side: Growth

For much of the quarter-millennium history of economic growth, progress was measured by how much stuff was made, by more goods per person. Today, goods are less important than services, and quality is more important than quantity, so the growth of quality has replaced the growth of quantity as the basis for increases in well-being. Yet it is very hard to measure services, and almost impossibly hard to measure quality.

A more general point is that GDP is much worse measured than is suggested by its cultural prominence. Gross concepts make no allowance for the depreciation or destruction of capital. There are both conceptual issues—no value is attached to nontraded services, the most important of which is unpaid work in the home, or to leisure—and practical issues—assumption-based estimates ("imputations" rather than measurements) that play an increasing role (up to one-third of household income) in advanced economies. There are good reasons for current practice, and almost equally good reasons to change. In the meantime, the magnitude of conceptual and practical uncertainty is large and growing, and we should treat the declining growth measures with a good deal of skepticism.

The output of many services is hard to measure, so the statisticians do what they can and measure inputs, not outputs. They make productivity adjustments—within each country's national accounts and among countries when making international comparisons—but these are imputations with large margins of error. In many cases, such as government services, productivity growth is ignored. Exceptional productivity growth in services goes largely unmeasured. One of the most important services—the benefits that owners get from living in their own homes—is almost entirely imputed, often by extrapolating from small and unrepresentative rental markets or by imputing the user cost of the asset. Technical improvements that make our homes better consumption machines go largely unmeasured.

While there is no evidence of systematic understatement of service growth, this is not true for improvements in quality or for the benefits of radically new goods. Many quality improvements and new goods are patched in to the national income accounts, and many scholars have argued that the benefits of the major consumer innovations of our time—ATMs, cell phones, e-mail, Internet shopping, personal entertainment devices—are seriously underestimated. No one knows how to fix this, and statistical offices make some allowances for improvements in quality in existing devices, like cars and computers, but the growth in material living standards is almost certainly being underestimated by the treatment of these items.

I also challenge the proposition that the information revolution and its associated devices do little for human well-being. Many have documented the importance of spending time and socializing with friends and family, but this is exactly the feature of everyday life that the new communication methods work to enhance. All of us can remain in touch with our children and friends throughout every day, videoconferencing is essentially free, and we can cultivate close friendships with people who live thousands of miles away. When my parents said good-bye to relatives and friends who left Scotland to look for better lives in Canada and Australia, they never expected to see or talk to them again, except perhaps for a brief and astronomically expensive phone call when someone died. Today, we often do not even know where people are physically located when we work with them, talk to them, or play with them. We can also enjoy the great human achievements of the past and the present, cheaply accessing literature, music, and movies at any time and in any place. That these joys are not captured in the growth statistics tells us about the growth statistics, not about the technology. If they are belittled by those who do not use them, it tells us only to pay no attention to those who purport to use their own preference to pass judgments on the pleasures of others.

For most of the world's population, who do not live in the rich countries, there has been no slowdown in growth. Indeed, the more than 2.5 billion people who live in India and China have recently experienced sustained growth rates that are unparalleled in any country or period. Can we expect those to continue?

Indian and Chinese growth rates have slowed in the aftermath of the financial crisis and were likely overstated by the official statistics of both countries. While the slowing is likely a short-term effect, we should also remember that country growth spurts are rarely sustained as long as have been India's and China's, so perhaps they are due to stop. China's political regime is not one that will easily tolerate creative destruction, and its corrupt and extractive regime will increasingly be a drag on growth.

Even so, to go back to Keynes, there are fundamental reasons that India, China, and at least some other now-poor countries should grow rapidly in the future. Catch-up growth is easier than growth on the frontier; many new ideas, new devices, and new ways of doing things can be imported from abroad and do not need to be reinvented from scratch. And while such importation requires local innovation, adaptation (and destruction) that does not come for free, catch-up growth is easier and, in the right circumstances, can be much more rapid than the original growth. Even sub-Saharan Africa, which was the basket case of economic growth in the 1980s and early 1990s, is showing signs of revival. Some of this comes from higher commodity prices, which cannot be relied on for the long run, but some also comes from better macroeconomic management learned from abroad. If the West can wean itself off the destructive foreign "aid" that it is currently pouring into Africa, governance is likely to improve too, and growth will follow.

The Brighter Side: Health

American life expectancy has increased by about thirty years since 1900, though the annual rate of increase before 1950 was about twice as fast as the annual rate of increase since 1950. At the same time, life expectancy gaps between the rich and the poor world have narrowed. If we were to use some compound of life expectancy and income as a welfare measure—for example, per capita income multiplied by life expectancy—overall growth in rich countries has been slowing even faster than income growth alone, and poor countries have been catching up with rich countries. Or at least they were catching up except for those affected by HIV/AIDS, and we might hope that those countries will catch up again once the epidemic is controlled.

The slowing in the rich countries, and the catching up of the poor with the rich, are both mechanical features of life expectancy. Life expectancy is a convenient but essentially arbitrary measure of population health, and it gives much higher weight to deaths of children than to deaths of adults. So the decelerating growth in life expectancy cannot be taken to mean that the decline in all mortality rates is slowing down or that all mortality gaps between poor and rich countries are narrowing. As for the future, the slowing down in the rate of growth of life expectancy cannot be taken as a sign of things to come. There are real threats to future mortality decline— whether HIV/AIDS is controlled is one—but the deceleration of life expectancy is not one of them.

In both rich and poor countries, life is riskier in early childhood and in old age, with little risk of death in adulthood. But in poor countries today, as in rich countries in the past, the chance of dying in the first few years of life is much higher than it is in rich countries. About 50 out of every 1,000 children born in India die in their first year, close to the fraction who died in Scotland in the year that I was born (1945). In 2010, fewer than 4 out of every 1,000 infants died in Scotland, the lowest figure ever recorded and one of the lowest rates in the world. In rich countries today, death stalks the elderly. In rich countries in the past and in poor countries today, death stalks the young. In poor countries today, as in rich countries in the past, progress comes from reducing mortality among children. In the rich countries today, progress comes from reducing mortality among adults.

The first health improvements came (and in some places are still coming) from better public health—such things as clean water, sanitation, vaccination, and the elimination of pests that cause disease. These things can bring rapid falls in infant and child mortality, and life expectancy zooms upward. Once those "easy pickings"—at least for life expectancy—are gone, health improvements have to come from reducing adult mortality, which means reducing heart disease and cancer. There has been enormous progress in rich countries in reducing mortality from heart disease, and many middle-aged and elderly lives have been saved. This kind of progress does much less for life expectancy than progress in reducing mortality among children.

We can argue either way about whether the life of a newborn is worth more or less than the life of someone in middle age or someone in old age, but there can be no automatic presumption in favor of the simplistic view that saving more years of life is always the best thing to do. The slowdown in the rate of improvement of life expectancy is essentially a measure of success, not of failure. In the rich countries, we have largely disposed of the early life killers, which are the ones that have the big effects on life expectancy and have moved on to the next killers, which strike at older ages.

The real question for our grandchildren and their grandchildren is whether the progress in mortality reduction can be expected to continue. Once again, the sky is not entirely clear, but I believe that the answer is yes.

The current reduction in mortality from cardiovascular disease still has some way to go. Antihypertensive drugs are cheap and effective but require patients to have their blood pressure regularly checked by a physician, something that many people do not do. There are many lives here that can be cheaply saved. Smoking rates have come down among men and, with a lag, among women, so that the gap in life expectancy between women and men is now smaller than it has been for many years. If women continue to quit as men have done, many fewer of them will die from cardiovascular disease and lung cancer.

What about cancers other than lung cancer? The most important are breast cancer (primarily among women), prostate cancer (entirely among men), and colorectal cancer (among both men and women). In very recent years, serious progress has been made against all three of these cancers, driven by a combination of screening and new drugs, some developed in the traditional way, by trial and error, and some using new scientific advances in understanding how cancer works. Unlike mortality reduction through antihypertensive drugs, giving people aspirin after a heart attack, or smoking reductions, these treatments are expensive, and their widespread use could be limited by lower growth rates of income should those come to pass. But many scholars believe that over the next fifty years, we will see the progress against cancer that we have seen in the past fifty years against cardiovascular disease.

One of the deep reasons that health will continue to improve is that people want it to improve and are prepared to pay for the innovations, basic science, discoveries about behavior, drugs, procedures, and devices that support it. Innovations cannot be bought off the shelf and do not always come along when they are needed. But there is no doubt that urgency helps. As each disease is conquered, the next becomes the main target; no one cared about Alzheimer's when a quarter of the population did not reach its fifth birthday. But as life expectancy increases, these later-life diseases become priorities, and as people get richer, they will devote larger and larger shares of their incomes to dealing with them, so that spending rises faster than national income.

In poor countries, infant and child mortality remains a major curse, even if there has been enormous improvement over the past half-century. The children who die in these countries would not have died had they been born in rich countries, and to that extent, we should be able to prevent their deaths. They are not dying from incurable exotic diseases but from respiratory infections, diarrheal disease, and vaccine-preventable diseases, all of which have been eradicated among children in rich countries. So the potential for progress is enormous. Some will come through more wide-spread education, particularly of women, which brings a wider understanding of the germ theory of disease and its implications, like the need for hand-washing and for clean water.

The major roadblock here is not the availability of medicines, many of which are cheap and readily available, but the capacity of many governments to develop a system of maternal and child care that will bring known remedies to these children and their mothers. Much will depend not so much on economic growth in poor countries—China did much better in reducing child mortality before it began to grow, and the same is true in India to a lesser extent—but on improvements in state capacity and state commitment.

Apart from sub-Saharan Africa, most deaths in the world today are from noncommunicable diseases such as heart disease and cancer, not from the infectious diseases that have been the primary enemy for much of human history. As we have seen, cardiovascular disease mortality has fallen rapidly in rich countries and has done so based on cheap drugs and on smoking reduction. While the new cancer treatments may be difficult for public health authorities to afford in many nonrich countries, cost is not a consideration for aspirin or for diuretics, and we can expect to see a spread in treatment rates from both public and private providers around the world. Again, the constraint may be the rate at which adequate physician-based health systems can evolve (public sector) and be regulated (private sector).

The outlook for smoking rates in poor countries is less positive, if only because rising incomes will work to increase smoking and because tobacco companies are targeting consumers in some middle-income countries.

Even HIV/AIDS, which has wiped out the life expectancy gains of the past fifty years in several countries in Africa, is being tackled by the provision of antiretroviral drugs. Between 2003 and 2010, the number of people receiving these drugs in poor countries increased from under 3 million to more than 10 million. With luck, the epidemic will be history long before the century is up.

There are links from income growth to health improvements; better nutrition comes with more money, public health projects (water and sanitation) cost public money, and the pressure for innovation is both fueled and financed by rising living standards. Yet it is a mistake to think that income and health always march together. Catch-up health improvements, like catch-up growth, require modest innovation—more in process than in concept—and historically there have been many occasions where there were massive reductions in mortality—through antibiotics, water provision, and mosquito control—in places where living standards were stagnant. Policy matters too. When China decided to encourage rapid economic growth in the mid-1970s, it turned away from the public health measures that had been a successful part of the previous regime. When thinking about the future, we must not suppose that everything depends on economic growth, so that even if growth falters, there is nothing that guarantees it will bring down health with it.

The Brighter Side: Everything Else

Living standards mean little if people are not alive to enjoy them, yet for people who are alive, it is difficult to live a good life in deprivation and misery. So I have focused here on mortality and living standards. But there are many other aspects of the good life, and here too, there is hope for further improvement.

For example, health is more than just being alive, and there is evidence not just that people are living longer, but they are healthier when they are alive. Some of this is medicine—I have a hip replacement that has enabled me to live a full and active life that would have been impossible without it. Others have replacement knees or even replacement hearts. Cochlear implants are beginning to reduce the fraction of people who cannot hear. Cataract surgery restores sight to many.

Better nutrition and better disease environments in childhood have increased adult heights around the world. For more than a century, Europeans have been growing taller at about 1 centimeter for each decade, and the Chinese are currently growing taller at the same rate. Americans seem to have stopped growing, Indians have barely started, and Africans born in the 1980s were shorter as adults than those born a decade before. Higher incomes and better childhood health produce taller adults. Height seems to help people lead better lives, sometimes because taller people are stronger and can earn more. Childhood nutritional failure and childhood disease hold back not only physical growth but the development of the brain, so that people who have less disease and better nutrition as children have better cognitive function as adults. And indeed, measured IQs have been rising around the world.

Violence has fallen; people have much lower chances of being murdered than used to be the case. This improves not only health but also the quality of life for those who do not have to live in insecurity.

Democracy is more widespread in the world than was the case fifty years ago. Oppression of one social group by another is scarcer, whether women by men, homosexuals by heterosexuals, workers by capitalists, farm workers by aristocrats, one ethnic group or caste by another. People have greater opportunities to participate in society than has ever before been the case.

Education has been on the rise in most of the world. Four-fifths of the people of the world are literate compared with only half in 1950. There are areas of rural India where almost no adult women ever went to school and now almost all of their daughters do so. Yet once again, much remains to be done, particularly in Africa. But if people are indeed the ultimate resource, healthy, well-educated people living in an open society are the most valuable of all, and the ideas and innovation that come from them benefit everyone and are the basis for continuing economic growth.

Of course, none of these things can be expected to improve everywhere or to do so uninterruptedly. Bad things happen. Wars destroy, and positive political regimes can be replaced by negative regimes that can reverse many years of progress. Epidemics like HIV/AIDS can eliminate decades of health improvements. Yet I expect those setbacks to be overcome in the future, as they have been in the past.

Perhaps the major uncertainty, on a world scale, is whether it will be possible to deal with climate change. It is hard to be optimistic about any global agreement today, and perhaps there will have to be great suffering and destruction before people come together to make changes. I do not know how this will come about. But the forces for progress and for collective action against imminent danger are also strong, and I would put my money on their winning out.

3   The Cone of Uncertainty of the Twenty-First Century's Economic Hurricane

Avinash K. Dixit

Brilliant minds, including Niels Bohr and Yogi Berra, are supposed to have declared that prediction is very difficult, especially about the future. And I can safely predict that several contributors to this book will invoke that dictum. Then why are we doing it?

Speaking for myself, I have a mixture of motives. First, following in Keynes's footsteps and in the company of such distinguished fellow contributors is irresistible. Second, I will not be around to be ridiculed when my predictions go spectacularly wrong. Weather forecasters and prognosticators of financial markets have thicker skins; they blithely make new predictions every day even as their previous ones prove to be mistaken. I will have the safety of absence. Third, and most important, indulging in wild speculation is simply too much fun.

Weather forecasters do take some precautions. They usually attach a probability to their forecasts of "precipitation" and recognize that forecasts further out into the future have larger margins of error by showing "cones of uncertainty" around their projected paths of hurricanes. Economic forecasts should do likewise.

The hurricane analogy seems especially apt as I write this. The winds buffeting the world economy, assisted and in some respects even caused by policy follies, have already produced the Great Recession, with fears of more to come. Therefore, I shall begin in the hurricane-forecasting mode and suggest possible paths within its cone of uncertainty.

At least one prediction can be made with high confidence; think of it as the central path in the cone. On it, in the course of the next century, there will be several financial and economic crises. Each crisis will be preceded by a boom and by a state of euphoria, when almost everyone will believe that "this time is different; we have learned how to avoid crises, and have finally learned the secret of how to sustain the Great Moderation." When the crisis hits, policymakers everywhere will be shocked and unprepared. Their panicked responses will merely paper over the real problems and sow the seeds of the next crisis a few years down the line.

Another fairly safe prediction pertains to international coordination for policies on global public goods, especially precautionary measures to reduce the risk of catastrophic climate change and mitigate its consequences. Reaching and implementing agreements will remain problematic. Only the Germans and the Scandinavians will make promises in good faith and strive to fulfill them. Britain will try to emulate them but will not succeed. America will be honest about its domestic political difficulties and therefore promise little or nothing, drawing criticism from countries like France and Italy, which will sign anything and then do nothing. China and India will repeatedly declare good intentions, but their main priority will be economic growth, and they will be too distracted by their internal problems to do much about the environmental impact of their growth.

A large fraction of the world's electricity will continue to be generated by burning coal and oil, emitting greenhouse gases. Solar, wind, and tidal power generation will contribute much less. Nuclear fission power will go through cycles: periods of gradual increase followed by sudden setbacks after scary accidents to reactors. Fusion power has always been the technology of the future, and that will still be the case a century from now.

If the forecasts of global warming come true, the lack of international action will have some side benefits. The Northwest and Northeast passages in the Arctic will be ice-free, reducing transportation costs from East Asia to Europe and the U.S. East Coast. However, by then, the major component of trade flows will be up and down the western Pacific along the east coast of Asia, or perhaps across the Pacific to the affluent countries in South America. The majority of traffic on the famed Arctic passages of yore will consist of tourists retracing the paths of Roald Amundsen and Adolf Erik Nordenskiöld.

What about the extremes of the cone of uncertainty? The United States and Europe are on the right edge. Dysfunctional politics and continued adverse demographic trends will trap these former economic giants into relative mediocrity in the world. Their situation will be eerily reminiscent of many Latin American countries in the bad old 1970s and 1980s. From time to time, they may enjoy a little growth, but much of the time, their economies will stagnate while newly dynamic economies of Asia, and parts of South America and Africa, grow faster. Europe and America will remain burdened by debt, both private and public, and suffer periodic bouts of inflation and currency crises. International Monetary Fund (IMF) officials from the organization's shiny new headquarters in Singapore will send missions to Washington and Brussels, to discuss the terms and conditions for renewing loans. The American and European public will resent these heavy burdens. The Americans will insist on their constitutional right to enjoy all the latest new imported personal helicopters and holographic 3D-surround home theaters that put them right inside the action in the movie along with the actors. The value of U.S. output will be much less than the value of all this consumption, so the country will continue to run large deficits requiring continuous borrowing. That won't stop Americans from simultaneously complaining about other countries running the surpluses that they lend to the United States to enable Americans to consume so much! Europeans will hold frequent and noisy demonstrations to defend their Bacchus-given right to sit and drink ouzo (or vin de table, or tepid beer, or something else) all day. The governments, whose primary objective is reelection, will not defy the voters and therefore will not fulfill the conditions they pledge to the IMF. But after long and difficult negotiations, the IMF will roll over the loans anyway. The borrowers know full well that if you owe the bank $1 trillion, you are in the bank's power, but if you owe the bank $1 quintillion, the bank is in your power.[1]

In America, recurrent macroeconomic crises will be made worse by the loss of technological leadership, as governments controlled by or beholden to religious conservative forces forbid research on the frontiers of biotech and related areas. American education will continue to be squeezed between the demands of religious fundamentalists and teachers' unions; this will accelerate the decline. China gives us a grim example of long-term decline. It led the world in science and technology for centuries. Then some capricious decisions of its emperors to halt exploration, blind faith in its own traditions and superiority, and distrust of anything foreign to China led to stagnation and decline from which almost six centuries were needed to climb back.[2] For the United States, the twenty-first century will be just the beginning of a similar downhill slide.

A side effect of this decline will become good news for some: the United States will regain its position as a manufacturing economy.[3] As early as

2011, production of some mops and brooms was coming back to the United States from China. The Chinese did not want to be making these crappy plastic goods any longer; they wanted to move into more advanced and complex technological sectors. At least this reversal will create employment for the poorly educated and unskilled U.S. workers.

On the left edge of the cone of uncertainty we find China and India, whose inevitable and irresistible rise to world domination is being forecast so confidently today, in the early years of the twenty-first century. Regional and ethnic inequalities in each of these countries will explode into repeated civil conflicts. The police and armed forces needed to cope with this situation will take up large fractions of their governments' resources, leaving little for productive social expenditures or public investment. Major infrastructure projects will suffer from neglect, as well as damage from sabotage and terrorism in the civil conflicts. Foreign investment will dry up, and successful domestic firms will leave for less troubled foreign countries.

Some of the scenarios I have laid out can coexist; others are mutually exclusive. But even a few of them together present a frightening prospect. Halloween approaches as I write this, so the timing is fitting for raising fright. But my real purpose in depicting such nightmares is, of course, to shock readers and, I hope, set in motion some actions that will reduce the risk of turning these potential nightmares into reality. What, then, might be a dream scenario, and what actions might bring it about?

In my dream scenario, policymakers will have learned that crises are inevitable and that the most important measures to deal with them have to be put in place in advance, during the good times. In the early 2000s, copper prices were high and Chile's government coffers were flush. The finance minister at that time, Andrés Velasco, resisted pressure from numerous special interest groups to spend this windfall on their favorite projects; instead he built up a large reserve fund and was heavily criticized by all those groups. When the Great Recession hit the world in 2007, most countries got into serious deficit and debt problems and had to make deep cuts in all programs. Chile would have suffered more than most others as the price of copper plummeted. But Velasco was able to use the accumulated reserve fund to cushion the shock, and he became a hero overnight. He was quoted as saying: "Being a Keynesian means being one in both parts of the cycle."[4] In my dream scenario, this slogan will be posted in huge letters on the walls of treasury departments in all countries, and the actual practice of their fiscal policies will conform to it.

I have a dream that America's public schools will recover the quality and purpose they had in the first half of the twentieth century and will turn out high school graduates equipped with skills, not just self-esteem. And these high school graduates will have affordable opportunities to go on to acquire college education in subjects that matter—mathematics, natural sciences, engineering, and, dare I say, a little basic economics, instead of the easier song-and-dance majors that are popular among too many U.S. college students.[5] In other words, I hope America will recognize that education is mostly an investment good, not a consumer good. Schoolteachers will be well paid and will have the respect of their communities. They will be motivated and dedicated to their vocation. They will not be obsessed with preserving the jobs of everyone regardless of ability, enjoying short working days and short school years, and retiring early on handsome pensions. They will have good knowledge of the subjects they teach and will come mostly from the top third, not the bottom, of their college classes. The same hopes and dreams apply, although with varying degrees of emphasis, for most of the world that is rich in 2013.

In my dream world of 2113, there will be opportunities for individuals to take risks, exercise initiative, and innovate, getting rich if they succeed. These opportunities will be equally available to all. Although the outcomes will be unequal, the bottom of the distribution will be cushioned by a sturdy social safety net. This will consist of a simple, comprehensible, and relatively nonmanipulable set of policies, for example, a negative income tax that replaces all the complex set of welfare payments, plus health care coverage that, at a minimum, protects everyone against ruinous expenditures. Many in the United States will reflexively denounce this as socialism, but they should be reminded that something very similar was first and most persuasively advocated by that hero of the libertarian right, Milton Friedman.[6] My ideal safety net will be quite lean and not so generous as to allow people to idle in comfort forever. Most important, it will offer only a modest flat backstop income for everyone. It will not protect bankers any better than it does bakers. It will not give any special treatment to people who build or buy expensive houses in locations that are at risk from hurricanes and floods, or those who take out large mortgages and home equity loans in the expectation that house prices can never fall, or those who take other absurd risks expecting to keep any profits and unload losses on taxpayers. It will not subsidize farmers who incur large debts to buy land in boom times and then produce too much. My ideal health care system will refuse coverage to people who have demonstrably chosen lifestyles that are known to lead to health risks like cancer and diabetes for the treatment of which the rest of us would have to pay huge amounts. Herbert Spencer's motto, "The ultimate result of shielding men from the effects of folly is to fill the world with fools," will be written in large letters on the walls of all government departments that offer bailouts, subsidies, insurance, and all kinds of handouts.[7] Darwin Awards are given posthumously to people whose reckless and foolish actions helped improve the gene pool by removing themselves from it.[8] Similar awards should be designed for those whose reckless and foolish actions lead to their own or their company's financial death. Golden parachutes of CEOs should be designed not to open when they depart after disastrous reigns.

When designing and implementing my ideal safety net, governments will thoughtfully balance the needs of the short run and the long run. Short-run economic and political imperatives are real and should not be neglected, but they often lead to excessive stimulus spending, preservation of firms and industries that should be wound down, and so on. On such occasions, politicians and several economists appeal to the great man whose essay we are attempting to update here: "In the long run we are all dead." But in this instance the great man made a serious logical error; he should have said: "In the long run we are *each* dead."[9] At any future date, other people will be alive, and every ethical policymaker should pay due regard to their interests even if they do not have a voice in today's political contests.

Wealth and income at the top will not be allowed to get so distant from the middle of the distributions as to threaten the basic cohesion of the society. Even those who do not accept any moral or normative arguments for limiting inequalities of outcomes should accept the practical positive one: in the absence of any such limit, the risk of a social revolution that threatens the well-being of even those at the top is too great. With some reasonable limit, the masses will not have reason to think that the rich belong to a completely different society or a country-within-a-country, a *Richistan*.[10] An underlying unity, a belief, and an emotion among the nationals of each country that we are all American, Indian, and so on, and that ultimately we are all human and citizens of planet Earth, will remain. People will have enough empathy with others to support them in times of need. However, they will also retain enough individuality and a sense of personal achievement, in short enough of the spirit of the much-maligned *Homo economicus*, to defy those social norms and customs that enforce conformity and stifle innovation, to go one's own way and be a maverick when the spirit moves one. Without such individualism, society can quickly become rigid and stagnant.

In my dream world, the political institutions of economic governance, and indeed politics as a whole, will be contentious but with civility and respect. People will debate others who hold opposite views but will not think that those differing views automatically make the others traitors or devil-worshippers or communists or whatever may be the favored condemnable category of the day. I believe that one of the most important ideas to emerge in the eighteenth century was that of "His Majesty's loyal opposition" in Great Britain. This recognized that the opposition in Parliament could criticize and challenge the actions of the government of the day without their basic loyalty to the monarch and the state being called into question. This permitted the scrutiny and dissent that was essential for the functioning of democracy and for reducing the risk of emergence of absolute rule or tyranny. Such loyal opposition, not only in legislatures but also from media, nongovernmental organizations, and other social groups, is more necessary than ever before in today's world, where control of information and technologies of coercion can put dangerously great powers in the hands of governments. I dream that we will all have several concentric circles of loyalty: to our family and friends, our social groups, our nations, our international organizations, and humanity as a whole. But we will all retain a spirit of loyal opposition, keeping those to whom we delegate some power of authority over us always on their toes.

How might my dream scenario be implemented? The ideal path would be one where everyone wakes up tomorrow morning, realizes what needs to be done, and contributes to bringing it about with a cooperative spirit and goodwill. But alas, the likeliest path is through a deep crisis. As Mancur Olson pointed out, reforms of institutions often come about after a war or some other crisis has dissolved the previously entrenched coalitions and destroyed the power of special interests.[11] Therefore, my dream scenario may follow one or more of my nightmare scenarios. My seemingly disconnected thoughts in this chapter may, after all, constitute a coherent narrative of the economic history of the coming century!

Will we move to a fifteen-hour workweek? Will we be another four or eight times as rich as we are now? Will we colonize the moon or Mars? I do not know and do not much care. I believe that the improvements in institutions and organizations that figure in my dream are much more important than any increases in leisure or any substantial increases in material wealth in today's first world. With good institutions, a good level of economic well-being can be sustained; without them, even great wealth can be fragile. I do hope that today's poor world catches up with the standard of living that prevails in many of today's advanced countries and that the currently rich countries retain their level of economic well-being. Advances beyond that would be nice, but they are not my biggest hope or concern.

4 Wealth and the Self-Protection Society

Edward L. Glaeser

Introduction

A century can seem like an enormously long time, but the contours of current America were in place 100 years ago. Per capita income in the United States was around $8,800 in 2012 dollars, about one-sixth of the current level. Cars, telephones, radios, and movies were new, but they were proliferating rapidly. The number of automobiles in the United States had increased tenfold from 1907 to 1913. The election of 1912 was a watershed, where the two most popular candidates had both embraced a vision of a far more active federal government, foreshadowing the changes that would occur after the New Deal.

Yet it still seems hazardous to say much about the future 100 years from now. Keynes's justly famous 1930 essay, "Economic Possibilities for Our Grandchildren," correctly foresaw a future that would be far wealthier than the bleak days of the Great Depression. Yet he incorrectly thought that this wealth would mean that "the economic problem may be solved" and that "for the first time since his creation man will be faced with his real, his permanent problem—how to use his freedom from pressing economic cares, how to occupy the leisure, which science and compound interest will have won for him, to live wisely and agreeably and well." Keynes imagined this prosperity could engender an ethical revolution where we could "return to some of the most sure and certain principles of religion and traditional virtue—that avarice is a vice, that the exaction of usury is a misdemeanor, and the love of money is detestable, that those walk most truly in the paths of virtue and sane wisdom who take least thought for the morrow."

Even in the wealthiest countries today, human beings do not think that their economics problem has been solved. People still work long hours to

become wealthier, and 60 percent of Americans say that their personal economic situation is fair or poor.[1] Earning more money is seen as a far more
pressing problem than finding better uses of leisure time.[2] And Keynes's
view that wealthier countries would turn their back on avarice and usury
seems almost risible in the wake of the recent financial crisis and subprime
mortgage morass.

Keynes's essay reminds us of the perils of prediction, but the more important question is not what is likely to happen but rather what could go drastically wrong. Correctly assessing the potential threats to future prosperity
is likely to be the first step in addressing those threats. In this chapter, I
begin with a rather banal description of the most likely economic scene
that will greet our great-grandchildren in 2113. Like Keynes, I am optimistic
that growth will continue and that the world will be a far wealthier place in
100 years. It also seems likely that trends will continue to favor the skilled
and the fortunate, but the poorest tenth will still experience significant
increases in living standards.

Unlike Keynes, I am skeptical that increasing prosperity will engender
any fundamental shift in the avaricious character of humanity. Greed will
surely continue, and I suspect that Keynes's "most sure and certain principles of religion and traditional virtue" will appear even more passé in years
to come. This prognosis is less uplifting than Keynes's ethical optimism,
but there is still plenty to like about a wealthier world, even if it is no more
virtuous than our own.

There is some chance that things will go terribly wrong, and that the
world in 2113 will not be more prosperous than the world in 2013. The
largest risks are man-made destruction, such as wars and large-scale terrorism, and vast pandemics, which can spread more easily in a globally
connected world. We need to have less fear of natural resource shortages,
for rising prices have a profound ability to induce technological change
and inculcate thriftier behavior. Indeed, the largest natural resource danger
would occur if the government intervened to artificially keep resource costs
low. More generally, we should worry lest political institutions worsen in
the wealthy world and fail to improve in developing countries, for bad politics can do tremendous harm. Economic stagnation for the poorer members of the wealthy world is a threat, both intrinsically and because it could
help lead to further political problems.

A Wealthy and Unequal Future

Much that Keynes wrote about the economic future seems as true today as it was in 1930, and indeed, even more applicable to the wider world. Keynes emphasized the effects of the growth of capital, and humanity still invests vast sums in physical capital. In 2011, the ratio investment to gross domestic product was about 15 percent in the United States and over 48 percent in China.

Keynes paid less attention to human capital, but the link between education and economic success became far clearer over the course of the twentieth century. And even America continues to expand its stock of human capital. In 2011, more than 30 percent of Americans over twenty-five years old had at least a bachelor's degree, as opposed to 26 percent in 2001. While there has been some angst about the fact that those twenty-five to twenty-nine years old are less likely to have college degrees than those thirty-five to thirty-nine years old, that comparison is compromised by the fact that some people continue to get their degrees in their late twenties and thirties. The share of those twenty-five to twenty-nine year olds in the United States with a college degree increased from 28 percent in 2001 and 2006 to 32 percent in 2011.

The growth of the level of human capital elsewhere is even more dramatic. According to the Barro-Lee data, average total schooling in China increased from 4.9 years in 1990 to 7.5 years in 2010. India's educational attainment increased from fewer than 3.0 years of schooling in 1990 to 4.4 years today.

Keynes also emphasized that "technical improvements in manufacture and transport have been proceeding at a greater rate in the last ten years than ever before in history," and since Solow, economists have given technological progress a preeminent role in explaining economic growth.[3] It would be hard to rival the transportation breakthroughs of the 1920s, such as trans-Atlantic air travel and a vast increase in automobile accessibility, but we continue to make incremental improvements in transport. China has recently experienced a rise in automobile ownership that is just as striking as the U.S. growth in the 1920s.

There continue to be substantial technological improvements in manufacturing. The Bureau of Labor Statistics estimates that manufacturing productivity increased by 6.3 percent in 2010 and 2.1 percent in 2011. And improvements in the developing world can be far more extreme; Hsieh and Ossa "find that the [total factor productivity] of the median Chinese manufacturing industry grew at an average rate of 15% per year" between 1992 and 2007.[4]

Of course, the most remarkable breakthroughs today have been in information technology products that were almost unimaginable in 1930. Moore's law, which stipulates that the number of transistors on an integrated circuit doubles every two years, may eventually break down, but our progress in computing power still remains enormous. Even more impressive is the creative use of new applications of information technology, from portable consumer tools (like the iPad) to electronic social networks (like Facebook).

These innovations are so hopeful because in many ways, information technology makes innovation itself easier by easing the flow of ideas. Much research today uses tools like Google, JSTOR, Wikipedia, and STATA. Information technology enables experimentation and evaluation, which speed the creation of knowledge itself. It stores information to ensure that our stock of knowledge continues to grow, contributing to an ongoing increase in worldwide wealth.

How will this wealth change our lives? Keynes and Galbraith imagined future lives of leisure, but that has not particularly materialized. Labor force participation rates for men over age sixty-five has declined dramatically, from a 46 percent participation rate in 1950 to a 19 percent rate in 1980, but the labor force participation rate for this group has actually increased since then.

The labor force participation rate for men between thirty-five and forty-four years old has dropped from 98 percent in 1950 to 91 percent today, but that trend says more about difficulties at the bottom end of the income distribution than about leisure among the prosperous. Juhn and Potter show that there was barely any decline in labor force participation among well-educated, prime-age males between 1969 and 2004.[5] Labor force participation has dropped most dramatically for high school dropouts, especially African Americans. Moreover, there seems to be little change in hours worked, conditional on employment, for prime-aged males (between twenty-five and fifty-four years old) in the United States since the 1960s.[6]

There are several plausible reasons why Keynes's prediction of increased leisure does not seem to have materialized. Most obvious, the rising productivity of workers creates both an income and a substitution effect, and while the income effect pushes us to consume more leisure, the substitution effect—the fact that labor is more remunerative—pushes us to work harder. Furthermore, it can be plausibly argued that technological changes have made work much more pleasant than it once was and that we have taken our increased wealth in the form of less painful jobs rather than in the form of jobs with fewer hours. A final hypothesis is that Keynes underestimated the ability of technological innovation to produce ever more interesting products to purchase.

In the case of women, the trend has overwhelmingly been toward more labor force participation and longer hours in the formal workplace. But that trend has been enabled in part by technological improvements that have decreased the hours needed for core tasks in household production. Bianchi et al. report that married women in 1965 spent an average of 22.3 hours per week on meal preparation, meal cleanup, and cleaning clothes.[7] By 1995, the time spent on those three tasks had fallen to 8.6 hours per week. A technological revolution in the household—microwaves, washing machines, mass-prepared food—radically reduced the burdens of home production and enabled the mass entry of married women into the workplace.[8]

The rise in female labor force participation appears to have leveled off during the mid-1990s, and there has been little upward trend since then. In 1995, 62.3 percent of women with a child under six years old were in the labor force, and that figure was 63.6 percent thirteen years later. New technologies seem to be a much better substitute for time spent washing dishes than time spent caring for toddlers, and it is hard to see why rising incomes should necessarily lead to a reduction in demand for parental interactions with small children. Certainly the opportunity cost of time will rise, but so will the returns to parental investment. If early childhood investments have a particularly sizable impact on long-term human capital development, then rising returns to skill could well lead to a lower labor force participation for parents of young children because they perceive that their time with small children will reap ever larger economic returns.

The three largest uses of Americans time are sleeping (8.7 hours daily), working (3.2 hours daily), and watching television (2.83 hours daily). The fact that Americans now spend almost as much time watching television as working is one of the most radical changes since Keynes's own day. Given the time spent on television and the technologically intense nature of the medium, it seems quite possible that the recent technological change that has created the most benefit is the proliferation of cable channels. It is similarly possible that the most radical changes in people's lives over the next century will be in the area of home entertainment. It seems impossible to know if new technologies will lead to more solitary pleasures or more social connection (as with Facebook), or whether the important new technologies will be primarily sedentary or more active.

Of course, economists are more often focused on the impact of technology on work than on leisure, and there is a widespread view that as information technology connects the world, non-Western nations will continue along a path toward economic parity. Perhaps China will not be as wealthy as the United States in 2113, but it will surely be far wealthier than it is today, and so will India, Latin America, and sub-Saharan Africa. If this scenario is correct, we can look forward to a world that is far more prosperous and more equal than it is today.

If we really want to experience giddy optimism, we can hope that spreading wealth will also mean spreading democracy, for the correlation between wealth and democracy is well established. While teasing causality out of that correlation is difficult, Barro[9] seems to suggest that wealth leads to democracy.[10] Glaeser, Ponzetto, and Shleifer argue that education is the critical ingredient supporting sustainable democratic institutions.[11] If this view is correct, then a wealthier world may also be far more democratic.

While the world as a whole is likely to become more equal, as illustrated by Sala-i-Martin, it seems far less likely that equality will rise within individual countries, even if things go well.[12] There is little reason to suspect that the rise in returns to skill will diminish or that less able workers will find fantastic job opportunities in a world where technology provides a close substitute, not only for much manual labor but also for personal services. Increasing technological sophistication may ensure that much manufacturing remains in wealthy countries, but that manufacturing seems likely to be light on labor. Labor-intensive production of tradable goods will surely continue to move toward poorer places.

The United States has experienced periods of wage compression, such as the middle decades of the twentieth century, but it seems unlikely that these conditions will reappear. Goldin and Margo primarily associated this wage compression with "a rapid increase in the demand for unskilled labor at a time when educated labor was greatly increasing in number."[13] Given the much higher levels of education today, it is harder to imagine any similar spurt in the numbers of educated workers. Given our current ability to substitute technology and capital for unskilled labor, it is hard to see how a spurt in demand for less skilled labor might materialize.

It is easier to imagine large-scale political interventions to reduce inequality than any economic shift that leads wages for the less skilled to rise dramatically faster than wages for those with the most human capital. It is possible that these interventions take a benign form, with smart investments in education and policies that reward works, such as the earned income tax credit. Yet it is also possible to imagine far worse interventions that would discourage innovation and entrepreneurship with high levels of taxation and discourage working among the poor by excessively rewarding economic inactivity.

Low-skilled labor in services and retail trade seems likely to continue to face competition from technology. In the United States, employment growth after the downturns of 1979 to 1982 expanded heavily in retail trade and services. The relatively jobless recoveries during more recent recessions reflect in part more meager employment expansion in these sectors, perhaps because of technology and logistics, like Internet retailing, that can substitute for less skilled workers.

High wages will not be limited to people with technological expertise, and there will continue to be high rewards within many service occupations. High-end hairdressers and limousine drivers and clothing salespeople may well thrive in a more technologically intensive world. I cannot imagine a world where wealthy people are unwilling to pay for pleasant interactions with a capable service provider. But the ability to provide such pleasant interactions is also a skill, and that skill is unevenly distributed across the population.

If income inequality continues and increases, it is quite possible that a larger fraction of the population will find themselves not working. America may have ended "welfare as we know it," but we continue to have a safety net that provides support for people who do not work. Nearly 9 million workers currently receive disability insurance, and the Bureau of Labor Statistics estimates that 10.5 million people aged sixteen to sixty-four are disabled and out of the labor force. The rapid growth in the numbers of disabled workers seems to reflect changing standards of admission to the disability insurance program (especially related to back pain and mental issues) rather than any increase in the perils of the workplace.

If salaries for less skilled workers remain relatively low and if a wealthier society provides increasing levels of support for not working, then it seems quite likely that we should expect to see a larger fraction of the population without jobs. Juhn and Potter report that the labor force participation rate for prime-aged males without a high school diploma fell from 94.6 percent in 1969 to 82.8 percent in 2004, while the similar figure for college graduates remained at 95.2 percent in 2004.[14] Data in the 2011 Current Population Survey, including all men over the age of twenty-five, shows an employment-to-population ratio of 50.9 percent for high school dropouts and 77.8 percent for college graduates.

The exit of many less skilled people from the workplace, especially those who are receiving disability payments, is not a happy thought, yet it seems to be an inevitable result of income inequality and social insurance. If unemployment causes skills to deteriorate or if disability insurance requires recipients not to work, then we can expect to see a permanent class of nonworking adults. A wealthy society will be able to bear the costs of the social insurance for this group, but given the strong link between self-reported life satisfaction and employment, they will remain an unhappy part of a rich world.[15]

The best chance for America in 2113 to avoid rising income inequality and the associated economic inactivity is for the education sector to become significantly more efficient at delivering human capital to poorer children. At this point, it is not obvious that public education has enjoyed many significant productivity improvements over the past forty years, making it an extreme outlier across U.S. industries. It seems more likely that this paucity of innovation reflects on the nature of public monopolies rather than on any inherent problems of innovating in schooling. The positive results experienced by many charter schools suggest that in some cases, competition can create really significant improvements in educational outcomes.[16]

Can a more competitive schooling system turn into a dynamo for producing improvements in education productivity and reducing inequality? An abundance of recent research finds that educational outcomes, including adult earnings, can be improved by hiring and retaining more able teachers.[17] Many scholars of charter schools attribute their success to substantially longer school hours.

But these two channels—better teachers and longer school hours—carry large costs and seem more likely to shift the level rather than the growth of education productivity. There are natural limits on the number of hours that we can reasonably expect students to be in school each day, and high-ability teachers will become significantly more expensive in a world that values skills because of their ability to undertake other tasks.

Only technological change offers the possibility of permanently increasing the growth rate of educational productivity and reducing inequality. There is a great deal of experimenting with new technology for education today, such as using online tools for teaching math. The ability to engage students and cater to their individual needs suggests real potential. Yet we lack the randomized trials and longer-term results that would demonstrate effectiveness among disadvantaged populations.

Because we have little guarantee that new technologies will ensure that human capital and prosperity spread widely throughout every population, we have every reason to expect that the world will continue to see large differences in income. This inequality is certainly unattractive from a Rawlsian perspective, and researchers have connected inequality with higher homicide rates, worse health outcomes, and even unhappiness.[18]

A highly unequal future is not all bad. Great fortunes can fund philanthropy, and we should expect plenty of that. Inequality of wealth provides plenty of incentives to work hard and innovate even in a more prosperous world. Still, inequality is one likely by-product of a wealthier world built on technology and human capital.

Increasing Wealth and Humanity's Moral Character

Will increasing wealth change the character of our citizens? Keynes boldly predicted that greed and materialism would become less prevalent in a more prosperous future. Keynes predicted that we "shall honour those who can teach us how to pluck the hour and the day virtuously and well, the delightful people who are capable of taking direct enjoyment in things, the lilies of the field who toil not, neither do they spin," but that does not seem to have come to pass. We certainly honor those who provide us with entertainment. Oprah remained the most admired American woman in the 2011 Newsweek Poll, but she has certainly toiled for her fortune.

There is perhaps somewhat more demand for people who will teach happiness, as well as economic success, and this may be a natural result of a wealthier world. There is every reason to suspect that happiness is a normal good. Yet attempting to avoid despair is not the same as living "virtuously and well." Everyone certainly wants to feel virtuous, but that can be accomplished more easily by lowering ethical standards than by increasing ethical behavior.

There has been modest growth in employment in socially conscious organizations that seem to offer a lifetime spent doing good. Between 1998 and 2009, employment in industries classified as "religious, grant-making, civic, professional and like organizations," rose from 2.49 million to 2.76 million, a 10.8 percent increase, which distinctly exceeds the national employment growth rate of 5.9 percent. The overwhelming share of the growth in this sector, which is overwhelmingly nonprofit, occurred in religious organizations, where employment grew by 220,000. The fastest growth rate has been in areas such as environmental, conservation, and wildlife organizations, which roughly doubled in employment, from 32,000 to 60,000, and human rights organizations, which expanded from 18,000 to 30,000. Yet while these sectors are growing, outside of the traditional religious sector, they remain a tiny fraction of the overall economy.

My own guess is also that no matter how wealthy humanity may become, we will remain the same types of creatures, with roughly the same mix of good and bad. From the perspective of traditional morality, I suspect that increasing wealth will do rather little to ameliorate any of the traditional seven deadly sins: greed, envy, sloth, gluttony, lust, pride and wrath.

Keynes seems to have thought that increasing wealth would lead to a radical drop in the marginal utility of more wealth, which would cause leisure to become relatively more valuable. In a sense, he is predicting that greed will decline, perhaps along with envy as well, and perhaps we would come to see a little more sloth. Naturally such an outcome is not even implied in the simplest model, where rising wages have both income and substitution effects, and empirically they seem to combine so that rising wages typically mean more, not fewer, hours of work.

But over time another large effect further works against Keynes's visions of leisure. New technology does not just mean better ways of producing old goods; it also means a dizzying array of new products. While we may reach diminishing returns in our consumption of old goods, the new goods continue to deliver new pleasures. Perhaps we should think of ourselves as having Dixit–Stiglitz utility functions, which are concave in each individual product, but where innovators constantly deliver more and more products, causing the overall function to become more and more linear. As long as there are sleek new iPads and shiny new shoes, I see little chance that humanity will stop desiring wealth any time soon.

While Keynes liked the idea of added leisure, enemies of sloth will perhaps be heartened by the fact that humanity will still be willing to work hard to earn more wealth. The antisloth crew should probably be most worried about the increasing levels of economic inactivity among the less educated. If that trend continues, abetted by rising inequality and a reasonable safety net, we may well see an increasing fraction of the population engaged in lives of limited work effort.

Envy similarly shows few signs of disappearing. A vast industry is engaged in giving people peeks into the lives of more financially fortunate. People rarely admit to envy. Survey evidence finds that more than half of Americans say that "having children" or "having enough free time to do the things you want to do" is very important to them, while only 13 percent admit that "being wealthy" is such a high priority. Yet it is hard to know if this survey reflects people's true desires rather than what they are willing to admit, or whether this represents any sort of trend.

Certainly one interpretation of the recent anger toward the wealthy, evinced in both surveys and events like the Occupy Movement, suggests a surge in envy. Research finds that people do say that they are less happy when they are surrounded by people who are richer than themselves and envy is one interpretation of that fact [19] I suspect that increasing wealth will not eliminate envy, as long as there is an abundance of far wealthier people with lifestyles that give them many advantages that are not available to ordinary people.

What about gluttony and lust, the two more physical sins? High obesity levels seem to suggest that gluttony is alive and well.[20] When it comes to obesity, we are in a race between two technologies.[21] The food industry comes up with increasingly time-efficient ways to consume tastier products, and the diet industry comes up with ways to lose weight. During much of the post–World War II period, the technological innovations of the food industry, including fast food and microwave ovens, appear to have dominated, and we ate more as a result.

Yet this trend does seem to have slowed since 2000, suggesting perhaps that improvements in diet technology have finally caught up.[22]

Technological innovations will try to produce tasty new products that do less to expand our waistlines, since that is what people want. I doubt that medieval theologians would have thought that gluttony is gone if the country is filled with people gorging themselves on delicious low-calorie products that do not make us fat, but there will be less of a public health risk.

Will rising wealth and new technologies also mean changes in lust, or at least extramarital sex? One cohort-level analysis found that premarital sex occurred earlier, and perhaps more often, between cohorts born in 1944 and cohorts born in 1974 and a leveling off after then.[23] The General Social Survey reports that the share of adults thinking that extramarital sex is always wrong has risen by about 10 percentage points since the 1970s, from around 70 percent to around 80 percent. Trends in actual infidelity are harder to ascertain, but there is little evidence supporting any large scale-change in behavior, and the best evidence suggests an overwhelming tendency toward monogamy in the United States.[24]

One reasonable view is that changes during the 1960s eliminated technological and legal barriers to premarital sex and divorce and that these events caused a shift in behavior that included more premarital tax and, temporarily, far more divorce.[25] But these shifts seem to have created a level effect, not any shift in the growth rate of such behaviors.

Moreover, AIDS made extramarital sex less attractive, and the threat of other sexually transmitted diseases remains. Rising returns to skill make the returns to investing in children higher, and some evidence suggests that divorce reduces education and earnings outcomes for children.[26] I suspect that lust will be no more or less prevalent in our grandchildren's generation than in our own.

When it comes to wrath, I concur with the view of Steven Pinker that human existence is steadily becoming less violent, and I suspect that this trend will continue.[27] America's cities are much safer than they once were. But these reductions in violence reflect improvements in the technology of policing and the political choice to radically increase the amount of incarceration, not any change in our temperaments. We are safer, but I am far from sure that there is any change in our moral character.

Some old hatreds seem to have dampened—racial animosity and anti-Semitism are far weaker forces in the West than they once were—but humanity's capacity to hate seems to be as deep as our ability to love. Our success as a species in large part reflects our ability to form groups that collaborate and fight against outsiders. Our deep tendency to form mental divisions between in-groups and out-groups will always mean that we will be susceptible to stories about the threats posed by outsiders, and those stories can easily evolve into hatred.

Glaeser discusses the impact of new technologies on the spread of group-level hatred.[28] As it becomes easier to spread stories, the supply of hatred becomes easier. But simultaneously these new technologies make it easier to rebut old stories as well. Many have expressed the fear that the possibilities for customized content made possible by the Internet will lead to greater ideological segmentation, but empirical evidence suggests that Internet users are actually exposing themselves to more, not less, ideological diversity.[29] Given these two offsetting trends, it is hard to predict that there will be either more or less hatred in decades to come.

We finally come to pride, which is often seen as being the greatest sin, because pride puts personal ambitions ahead of moral constraints. While some psychologists argue that self-esteem has risen dramatically and created a "Generation Me,"[30] others argue that the observed changes are fairly small.[31] One analysis of lyrics in popular songs found increased use in words such as I and "me" over the period 1980 to 2007, which perhaps can be interpreted as an increase in narcissism.[32]

Why should we expect self-esteem or narcissism to rise over time? One interpretation is that technological changes and increasing wealth have made it increasingly possible to purchase key services in a market, and not to rely on social connections or group membership, such as membership in fraternal organizations.[33] These changes may have caused parents to increasingly emphasize individual achievement and put less emphasis on the self-deprecation that is often helpful in group situations. If these trends continue, it would be surprising to see any significant decline in pride.

From the perspective of these traditional sins, it is hard to see much promise of a more moral future. Keynes's vision was rosy, but little in the past eighty-three years has supported his views. Looking forward, it seems likely that our grandchildren will still hate and envy, still battle with gluttony and lust, and, if anything, have even more self-esteem, at least if our world continues to become wealthier and better at catering to individual whims. Yet there are threats that could cause a significantly less benign world future.

Where Be Dragons? Threats to Future Prosperity

A world of increasingly widespread wealth and prosperity is not inevitable. There are certainly known and unknown hazards that are man-made and natural that could derail the relatively upbeat scenario discussed thus far. Keynes was writing when the economic costs of the Great Depression were far from evident. Even less clear was the cataclysmic world war that would come. A major power conflict is still possible, and it could wreak even more damage today than it did during the 1930s. Weapons of mass destruction have increased the dangers posed by rogue states and terrorists. Moreover, natural disasters, including those potentially linked to climate change and contagious diseases, also have the capacity to cause enormous harm. We could also experience a political collapse that could eliminate economic freedom and protection of property. These problems are not themselves economic, but they might cause so much damage that our grandchildren would occupy a world that is no wealthier than our own.

Indeed, a child born, as my father was, in the year of Keynes's address, spent almost all of his life in the shadow of major power Armageddon. First, there were the extreme conflicts that began with Japan's invasion of Manchuria, which lasted from 1931 to 1945. After 1945, the Cold War, and its occasional hot progeny, loomed over the world until the fall of the Berlin Wall forty-four years later. For most of those years, a nuclear holocaust seemed like a real, if remote, possibility to almost everyone, and it always seemed possible that our grandchildren, if they survived such a war, would live on a radioactive planet that was far poorer than our own.

The threat of major power conflict has seemed far less likely since 1989, but some threat surely remains. Russia is still well armed, and China is the more rapidly growing power. The utter destruction that would come from a major power war has seemed like the best protection against the start of such a war, but that assumes that reasonable leaders will hold power. It is conceivable that unreasonable men, like those who led Germany and Japan during the 1930s, will once again come to control a major power.

Despite America's occasional penchant for starting smaller wars, it is hard to imagine that America's democratic process would produce leaders eager to start another world war. Russia is somewhat democratic. Its current leadership may occasionally be bellicose, but again there seems to be little interest in gambling everything on major power warfare. China's leaders do seem committed to regaining control over Taiwan and other areas of former Chinese influence, but Chinese leadership appears both quite patient and fairly rational.

The larger threat would seem to come from a major shakeup in the political structure, possibly of either Russia or China. China's increasing prosperity and urbanization could well lead to a massive surge for democracy. A major Chinese downturn could also produce an uprising. At best this surge could lead to a peaceful transition and the creation of the world's most populous republic. Yet such transitions have often been jerky, and failed transitions to democracy have often led to military or other dictatorial coups. Hitler himself represented right-wing revulsion with the transition to Weimar democracy.

Given the extreme uncertainty of such a transition and the natural tendency of overly optimistic leaders to rise to the top during periods of chaos, the world could be at risk. We may hope that Russia's transition to democracy is permanent and that China will either steadily evolve toward democracy or at least remain stable, but it is hard to completely forget that Mao once declared, "No matter what kind of war breaks out—conventional or thermonuclear—we'll win," because even if "we may lose more than 300 million people. So what?"

The threat of highly destructive individuals leading either rogue states or terrorist groups is even higher, and weapons of mass destruction make it possible for even smaller entities to create enormous destruction. Repeated nuclear strikes on large cities would create enormous direct destruction and possibly lead to a breakdown in trade and commerce that would derail us from the path toward increased prosperity. Yet with twelve years of hindsight after the September 11, 2001, attacks on the World Trade Center and the Pentagon, there has been more resilience than vulnerability.

Those attacks were indeed a reminder of just how much damage could be caused by an organization with members who were willing to die. The September 11 terrorists were armed with nothing more high tech than a box cutter, and yet they were able to strike at two hugely symbolic American buildings and kill thousands. Still, the economy and even downtown New York City moved onward with barely a sputter.

It is easy to imagine that future terrorists, perhaps armed by rogue states, will do even more damage to a major population center. America may have invested more in security, but given the abundant supply of people angry with the United States, continuing attacks appear inevitable. Eventually a larger-scale attack seems likely to hit, causing enormous harm, but unless the terrorist acts are able to destroy wide swaths of urban America or Europe, the West should be able to come back, just as it recovered from September 11 and World War II.

Natural disasters may be harder to gauge, but unless they are almost global, and only pandemics have historically been that large, they seem likely to cause much localized suffering but not widespread economic distress. Cyclones, earthquakes, and floods represent one class of disaster, which has caused hundreds of thousands of fatalities. However, Kahn documents that these disasters have much higher death tolls in poorer countries, perhaps because wealthier countries have better infrastructure and more competent public sectors that can better respond to the crisis.[34]

The protective effect of greater wealth and technologies that protect and predict suggests that a wealthier world is likely to be a safer world, although there are at least two countervailing forces. First, development can mean the use of dangerous technologies, like nuclear reactor plants, that can magnify the impact of a natural disaster, as Japan's tragic 2011 experience makes plain. Second, it is possible that changing climate conditions will make extreme events more likely and increase sea levels generally, increasing flooding risks.

Still, while such disasters may cause great harm, historically these events have been localized and limited in their long-run impact. Extreme cyclones tend to be tropical phenomena, and earthquakes disproportionally strike on fault lines. In the past two centuries, there are few cases of countries whose long-run growth has been seriously set back by an earthquake, cyclone, or flood.

By contrast, pandemics have done far more damage. At least three times in history, outbreaks of contagious disease have killed over 25 million people and perhaps as many as 100 million. The first two disastrous outbreaks were the plague of Justinian in the sixth century and the Black Death eight hundred years later. The plague of Justinian is arguably the most catastrophic natural disaster in human history, because its huge death tolls were accompanied by a profound weakening in the Roman and Persian empires, and their declines can be seen as the harbingers of centuries of political chaos and economic stagnation.[35] The Black Death, by contrast, seems to have created far less political dislocation, and if anything, it led to rising wages by improving the land-labor ratio in workers' favor.

Bubonic plagues themselves are unlikely to cause widespread destruction today. We have antibiotics that can fight the disease and, more important, far less of humanity comes in contact with rats that can carry infected fleas. Indeed, humanity has been relatively effective at reducing the impact of insect-delivered disease in the wealthy world, often with vector control that destroys the habitats of the most dangerous disease transmitters.

Public health advocates have worked to ensure the geographic separation of humans from rats and other animals that provide homes to fleas. Malaria and yellow fever were checked by eliminating the bodies of standing water that allowed mosquitos to breed. Massive investments in clean water were also effective in reducing the threat of waterborne diseases.[36] While AIDS has killed approximately 35 million people, the deadliness of sexually transmitted disease will always be limited by the ability of humans to protect themselves through abstinence and monogamy.

It would seem that the biggest potential for a future pandemic comes from airborne diseases such as influenza. The 1918–1919 influenza pandemic seems to have killed between 50 million and 100 million people, creating a death toll exceeding that of World War I. The ready ability of flu viruses to mutate limits our ability to ensure protection through medication. Troop movements helped spread the 1918 pandemic, and the highly connected nature of the world means that these viruses can spread rapidly throughout the globe.

Yet there are also reasons to be optimistic about our ability to counter any future pandemic. We have a vast amount of medical knowledge that may help us to quickly understand the nature of the disease, if not to develop a cure. That knowledge should presumably support protective strategies, including quarantine and face masks, to prevent the transmission of the disease. We certainly cannot be sure that we will prevent the death of millions, but unless the disease infects with extraordinary rapidity, we should be able to act quickly enough to prevent a cataclysm on the level of 1918. Moreover, our economies recovered relatively rapidly from that setback as well.

Famines represent the last major class of natural disaster. They have some similarity to other natural resource crises, including energy shortages, but the food supply, unlike the supply of oil, coal, and minerals, is dependent on weather conditions, and that creates significantly more vulnerability. Yet the general trend in food production is that humanity is producing more and more goods using less and less land. Improvements in technology are making it ever easier to feed billions, and the variability of food production in wealthy countries has been relatively low.

The harbingers of doom have proven to be completely wrong in their predictions of food-related disaster due to overpopulation.[37] The declining amount of land being used in food production suggests that it would be quite possible to increase food production, if need be, and we could also switch from forms of consumption that are far more grain intensive (like meat) to direct consumption of basic grain products in any emergency. Shortages would lead to rising prices, as long as the government does not respond with food price controls and agricultural producers would respond.

Moreover, the vast size of the world and its geographic diversity limit the potential impact of long-term climate change. It is certainly possible that global warming could worsen agricultural conditions in sub-Saharan Africa. Yet long-term climate changes would also presumably have a more positive effect on the vast amounts of land in Canada and Siberia that could be used far more intensively if they became warmer.

The famine risk lies not in long-run trends but in short-term shocks, and climate change could possibly cause such shocks to become more severe. Historically, famines tend to reflect a combination of farming and politics: a temporary shock combines with a political system that fails to deliver aid to the starving.[38] The most extreme famine event appears to have been the Great Chinese Famine from 1958 to 1961, where more than 30 million people perished. China also had millions of deaths from famines in 1927, 1929, and the early nineteenth century.[39] The Soviet Union experienced millions of deaths from famines in 1921–1922, 1932–1933, and 1946–1947. There were also extremely large famines in Bengal in 1943, Bangladesh in 1974, Cambodia in 1975–1979, and North Korea in 1995–1999.

The prevalence of famines seems to have become essentially nonexistent in the wealthy world. Europe saw its last famine more than sixty years ago, and even the horrors of the Great Chinese Famine are a full half-century in the past. Even if individual countries have terrible harvests, the diversity of weather throughout the world has kept the world's grain output relatively stable. As long as countries have either the wealth to buy grain from elsewhere or the ability to tap into humanitarian aid (unlike North Korea in the 1990s), famine seems likely to pose less and less of a threat.

There seems to be even less risk that humanity will face crises due to shortages of other natural resources, since these are enduring stocks rather than flows produced through a combination of weather, soil, and human inputs. There have been fears of running out of oil since the 1970s, and there has been a more current scare surrounding shortages of phosphorus, the critical ingredient in fertilizer.[40] Water is also occasionally discussed as a scarce natural resource, and rare earths that are used in batteries and other electronics could be in short supply.

While there is a perpetual market for articles trumpeting doomsday scenarios, conservation, innovation, and substitution all tend to work against dire outcomes. The natural forces of supply and demand mean that as demand outstrips supply, prices will rise, and in response, consumers will restrict their purchases of the commodity. Thirty years ago, Honda Civics got more than fifty-five miles per gallon on the highway, and these would have surely become more prevalent if gas prices had stayed high. The intervening decades have only increased the options for fuel-efficient cars, which represent one natural response to higher gas prices. Similarly, higher phosphorus prices should translate into higher food prices, which will lead to less consumption of fertilizer-intensive foods like meat.

The steady improvement in fuel-efficient cars reminds us that innovation provides a second response to natural resource shortages. This innovation can take the form of producing more resource-efficient devices, like high-mileage cars, or producing products that eliminate the need for the resource altogether, like electronics that do not depend on particular rare earths. We may end up with far more efficient solar panels and more efficient desalination plants for water. Humanity's track record in responding to shortages with innovation has been impressive and is likely to remain so.

Finally, there is the potential for substitution into alternative means of producing the same core service. Public transit can be used instead of cars. We can recycle phosphorus from human waste instead of mining. We can use coal instead of petroleum in electricity-generating plants.

It is certainly possible that some commodities we now experience as being cheap will be expensive for our grandchildren. There will certainly be commodities that are far more expensive for our grandchildren than they are today, just as there are commodities today that are far more expensive today than they were in Keynes's time (land near London, for example). But commodity shortages have not yet seriously bedeviled economic progress, and it seems that they will in the future.

I have mentioned already the political risks that might come from inequality—a society that taxes economic activity too much and subsidizes too much economic inactivity. But there are far worse outcomes than excessive egalitarianism. Perhaps the two biggest fears would be a break-down in basic property rights protection or an excess of regulation that sty-mies entrepreneurial energy. At this point, property rights are reasonably well protected in most of the developed world, although some developing economies are far from providing core legal services. Hyperinflation is one classic method of expropriation, but there is yet little danger of that. Excessive regulation of labor markets and business activities seems to stifle some of the economies in the developing world and also harms southern Europe.

I do not particularly expect the federal government in the United States to improve over time, but a doomsday scenario does not seem likely either. We have enjoyed basic political stability for 225 years, and lurches in one political direction have generally been followed by movements in another direction. The vast American debt certainly will create pressure for moderate inflation in years ahead, which will reduce the real value of our obligations, but although inflation does carry costs, there is little evidence that mild inflation radically reduces growth. I think that the biggest political danger is not some radical downward spiral, at least not in the United States, but rather an increasing orientation toward protecting the present rather than encouraging growth, a topic I turn to in the next section.

The two most extreme threats to future prosperity would appear to come from human destruction, caused by either major powers or an exception-ally well-armed and vicious smaller entity or contagious disease. Other natural disasters, such as earthquakes, cyclones, and floods, will certainly continue to cause great harm, but traditionally these disasters have been far too small to set back global economic growth seriously. Better technol-ogy and governance have the capacity to mitigate much of this danger. Famines or shortages in other natural resources seem even less likely to seriously retard growth because the price mechanism pushes toward ben-eficial behavioral responses, such as the technological innovation that can promote alternatives and efficiency.

The Self-Protection Economy

While it is reasonable to be concerned about these threats, fear itself can be a problem. Increasing prosperity means that people are increasingly satis-fied with the status quo and increasingly unwilling to risk change. While individuals may make appropriate private decisions about the right level of self-protection, there are more reasons to be concerned that the political economy process may lead to an excess of different forms of protection, which can be as disparate as defense spending, public health care, and regulations barring new buildings and business.

The basic economics of self-protection suggests that individuals will find it desirable to spend more on protection when they have more to lose. If an individual has wealth W and a probability P of losing that wealth, then P is a decreasing function of spending on self-protection, denoted S, and if the person is maximizing expected wealth, the person's optimization problem is to maximize $(1 - P(S))W - S$. This yields the first order condition $-P'(S)W = 1$, which describes a maximum assuming that $P''(S) > 0$, so that there are diminishing returns to protective spending. The implicit function theorem tells us that the derivative of spending on defense with respect to W will equal $-P'(S)/P''(S)W > 0$. The returns to spending on protection are proportional to the amount that we have to protect.

A similar result occurs if we are spending to stay alive. In this case, assume that $P(S)$ is the probability of death. Welfare for the living equals $U(W - S)$, where $U(.)$ is concave, and utility if dead is normalized to zero. In that case, individuals choose S to maximize $(1 - P(S))U(W - S)$, which yields first-order condition $-P'(S)U(W - S) = (1 - P(S))U'(W - S)$, and the derivative of spending with respect to wealth equals $-P'(S)U'(W - S) - (1 - P(S))U''(W - S)$ divided by $P''(S)U(W - S) - 2P'(S)U'(W - S) + (1 - P(S))U'(W - S)$. The two terms in the numerator capture the fact that rising wealth makes it more valuable to protect one's life and that rising wealth reduces the marginal utility of cash, which makes spending on self-protection less painful. The three terms in the denominator are all positive.

This basic logic suggests that richer people should spend more on insurance, automobile safety, and other investments that reduce the probability of death or losing a large proportion of their wealth. The Consumer Expenditure Survey tells us that households earning more than $150,000 spend twice as much, as a share of total expenditures, on insurance than households earning less than $70,000.[41] While an increasingly wealthy world will be increasingly concerned with protecting itself, there is nothing particularly worrisome about wealthier people buying more life insurance or safer cars. If anything, because there are externalities associated with dying (costs imposed on friends, loved ones, employers, and others), standard economics suggests that we probably underprotect as individuals rather than overprotect.

There is more chance that the public sectors will do too much to protect against change, and the costs of this protection can be both vast amounts of public spending and excessive limitations on innovation and change. In 1980, 49 percent of the federal budget (excluding net interest payments) went to five protection-oriented functions: defense, health spending, Medicare, disability insurance, and income security (excluding federal employee retirement benefits).[42] In 2011, 64 percent of the budget went to those five categories.

While the end of the Cold War was supposed to have delivered a peace dividend, America was spending 56 percent more, in real terms, on defense in 2011 than it was in 1991. It is possible that in the historical context, this defense spending will seem like an aberration caused by the wars of the past decade. But there is an alternative viewpoint: an increasingly wealthy society is willing to pay enormous sums to protect itself from external threats. Greater wealth also makes us willing to spend vast sums to limit the loss of American defense personnel, through a technology- and capital-intensive approach to national defense.

The increase in spending on "health" and Medicare can also be seen in this light. Just as the algebra above suggests, a wealthy America wants to spend more on investments that keep us alive and maintain our stock of health capital. Interestingly, we seem to have been willing, so far, to do this for both middle-income Americans, in the Medicare program, and for poorer Americans, in the Medicaid program. While there has been a strong backlash against some antipoverty programs, America has kept to the rule that poorer people are "entitled" to health care quality that is not that different from middle-income people, and that means that the health care expenditures for the poor also continue to increase.

Disability insurance expenditures have increased from 3 percent of the budget in1980 to 4 percent in 2011. In real dollars, disability expenditures increased over thirty-fold between 1960 and 2011. Again, this is easy to interpret as a wealthy nation paying to protect itself against the downsides of an adverse, life-changing event.

While Americans resolved in 1996 to end welfare as we know it, the share of federal spending on social insurance has not particularly declined, although current high spending levels reflect the economic downturn. Despite rising levels of obesity, the share of the after-interest budget spent on food stamps increased from 2.6 percent in 1980 to over 3 percent in 2011. Unemployment compensation, as a share of the budget, is about the same in both years, reflecting the fact that 1980 was also a year of economic troubles. The largest growth area has both "other social insurance," which also includes direct expenditures on disability aid (for those not covered by the social security trust fund), Temporary Aid for Needy Families, and the earned income tax credit.

While America is still vastly less prone to spend on social assistance than most other wealthy countries, we have become slightly more generous over time. Various forces, including our majoritarian government, robust checks and balances, and ethnic heterogeneity, have left the United States with far less of a welfare state than European nations.[43] Yet even if we remain less generous than they are, we are still likely to become more protective over time if we continue to become wealthier.

While federal welfare programs aimed at helping the very poor could become more efficient, this is not the area for expecting too much self-protection. In a majoritarian system, politics will always constrain transfers to a poor minority. The larger worries come from overspending on protection for middle-income Americans, such as Medicare, inappropriate activity in defense, and too much regulation that limits change and innovation.

The large increase in Medicare spending reflects both a program-specific design flaw and larger problems that are likely to make long-term reform extremely difficult. The key design flaw is that the program was designed to pay for any medical procedure without regard for cost. In 1965, there were a limited number of procedures, and so this issue seemed moderate. But the incentives inherent in that design unleashed the genius of American capitalism, and medical innovations have proliferated. There is a lot to like in the lifesaving technologies that have been created, but the program's design seems to imply that eventually all of GDP will be spent on new medical procedures.

In principle, it would be relatively easy to change the program's design to eliminate this problem altogether. Individuals could be issued health care vouchers, equal to current per capita spending on Medicare, which would increase at the rate of GDP. Representative Paul Ryan floated such a voucher plan in his proposed 2011 budget. But as we saw in the fight over

Obama's health care plan, there can be enormous antipathy toward taking away any middle-class benefits.

The larger structural problem is that the constituents for public health care spending include both providers and consumers, and today this group combines the 51 million Americans who are Medicare beneficiaries and the 15.3 million workers who are in health care (13.5 percent of all U.S. employment). Together, this means that more than 20 percent of Americans are beneficiaries of the Medicare system, giving it an extraordinarily widespread base of support.

Moreover, its supporters are disproportionately likely to vote and include extremely well-organized groups like the AARP (American Association of Retired Persons) and the American Medical Association. The size of this voting and lobbying bloc makes it easy to understand the enormous roadblocks barring significant reductions in the nature of the benefits level, even if those attempted reforms are trying only to freeze the level of benefits at current levels, not control the growth in costs that will come from new procedures.

Reforming the current policy is also bedeviled by two aspects of the status quo bias.[44] One part of the bias is that there are tremendous political challenges in breaking promises, like a commitment to unlimited medical procedures for older Americans. The human tendency to get angry at perceived losses motivates the beneficiaries of the current program. Paul Romer (1996) explains that this tendency explains why Franklin D. Roosevelt was so eager to ensure that social security would be structured as a promised entitlement.[45] A somewhat weaker tendency to feel bad about breaking promises limits wider enthusiasm for cutting back on promised benefits.

The second part of the status quo bias reflects beliefs about change. Individuals have few personal experiences that can enable them to objectively judge the impact of a proposed policy reform, and this makes them dependent on external assessments of any reforms, a dependence that makes it particularly easy for advocates to influence beliefs.[46] If the enemies of reform are far better organized than the friends of reform, as they are in the case of Medicare, then they will dominate the persuasion process and produce widespread fear of change.

Imperfect cognition may also lead to an excess of protective spending on national defense. The groups with the best information about threats to the United States are typically also those groups, like the Defense Department and the Central Intelligence Agency, that have the most to gain from defense-related spending. Moreover, it is probably easier to generate misleading evidence about bad intentions than to persuade people that outsiders are benign. If both good and bad actors or countries routinely send off neutral signals showing no malign intent, but only bad actors generate signals indicating a threat, then a few false benign signals will have far less of an effect on posterior beliefs (since they could have come from a malign power as well) than a few negative signals.

America's post-1941 track record has generally been to overstate the threat from other countries. Until Richard Nixon's rapprochement with China, we surely overestimated China's inclination to take military actions against the United States and our allies. In the 1970s and 1980s, we surely overestimated the threat posed by the Soviet Union. After September 11, 2001, we seem to have held exaggerated beliefs about the dangers posed by Saddam Hussein and Iraq. It seems likely that in years to come, we will continue to aggressively fund defense out of fear of foreign aggressors.

Fears are also part of a third element of the self-protective society: regulatory barriers to change. Since the 1960s, many parts of the United States have seen a regulatory shift where building, once relatively untrammeled, is beset by a dizzying array of land use restrictions.[47] The cost of these regulations is that there is too little building in high-demand areas and prices are too high. Glaeser and Ward estimate that in eastern Massachusetts, these regulations are far too high to be justified as means of maximizing total land value (one traditional test of Pareto optimality).[48] Glaeser, Gyourko, and Saks look at land use restrictions in Manhattan and similarly estimate that they are far too high to be socially optimal.[49]

There are also restrictions barring the entry of new businesses. Food trucks, for example, have been barred in some cities, including Detroit, because of fears that they will reduce the profitability of incumbent restaurants. Bertrand and Kramarz show that barriers to building new retail establishments in France seriously retard employment growth.[50]

Why are such regulations so popular? One theory argues that it is difficult to transfer rents from new entrants to incumbents because of political or legal barriers. As a result, incumbents do experience mild losses from change and do not experience any upside. Local politics favors incumbents because they have votes, while potential newcomers do not. Incumbent businesses may also have built up influence over time.

There is also a somewhat less rational explanation for NIMBYism. According to this view, incumbents believe that the change will do far more harm than it actually will. They are overestimating the losses from leaving the status quo, perhaps because interested parties have spread stories to that effect.

Rising wealth levels mean that incumbents have more to lose and will fight harder to oppose change. Moreover, incumbents will see less benefit in the added taxes that new businesses or residents might bring. Certainly the fight against new construction has been the most successful in the wealthiest parts of America, and perhaps more of the country will come to resemble those areas as the country itself becomes wealthier.

There is a logic to the self-protection society. A wealthy place has a lot to lose, and it naturally wants to protect its prosperity. Yet the political process, and potential behavioral ticks, means that wealthier countries can easily tilt toward overprotection. The downside of overprotection is that we spend too much on defensive measures, including Medicare and military defense, and put in place too many barriers to change. The result could be a country that is determined to hold onto what it has and increasingly unwilling to allow change. That could lead to a permanent decline in the level of technological change and economic progress.

Conclusion

I share the basic optimism of Keynes's vision. His view that our grandchildren will be far wealthier than ourselves seems as true in 2013 as it was in 1930. Yet unlike Keynes, I doubt that this wealth will lead to a radical decrease in hours worked for most Americans. After all, rising wealth also means increasing returns to labor. I am even more skeptical that added wealth will lead to any great moral shift in humanity's character, as Keynes once envisioned.

In Keynes's day, it seemed as if economic gains would be experienced broadly, but since then, globalization and new technologies have led to more inequality in the wealthy world, even if they make the entire planet a more egalitarian place. This inequality means that many Americans may not enjoy much of the fruit of our added prosperity. It also raises the risk of ultraegalitarian political policies that may compromise continuing economic growth.

A radical shift away from economic freedom is one of the risks that threaten our grandchildren's wealth. There are also threats from global violence and possible pandemics, which can now more easily spread from continent to continent. I recognize these risks but remain hopeful that we will avoid the worst outcomes. I expect that localized natural disasters, such as cyclones and earthquakes, will continue to do limited damage to the global economy, even if they do terrible damage to particular places. The threat of natural resource shortages seems far less pressing, since rising prices should elicit healthy behavioral responses.

One recurring fear is that this prosperity will produce a self-protection society, more interested in keeping what it has than in creating change. Humankind has become wealthier precisely because we have taken risks. Yet a society that exacts huge tax burdens to pay for health care and national defense, two key aspects of self-protection, and places large barriers to change seems to be embracing the past over the future. My belief in the future's potential makes me fear that we will go too far trying to protect what we have now.

Acknowledgments

I thank the Taubman Center for State and Local Government for financial support. Kristina Tobio provided her usual superb research assistance.

5 Keynes, His Grandchildren, and Ours

Andreu Mas-Colell

In 1930 John Maynard Keynes delivered a lecture entitled "Economic Possibilities for Our Grandchildren" at the Residencia de Estudiantes in Madrid. It was not a very characteristic piece for Keynes, whose better-known observation about the long term is that we will all be dead. Yet in the Residencia de Estudiantes, he put aside this extreme form of realism and spread the wings of imagination. His lecture caused "surprise, if not astonishment" to an audience that expected to hear his views on the economy of 1930.[1] That was not what they got. In a world in the first year of an unprecedented depression, Keynes chose to offer an optimistic, even idyllic, view of the future. He conjectured, for example, that 100 years from then, the standard of living in what he called "progressive economies" (which I assume meant the United States, Great Britain, and those countries that considered themselves as such) would be multiplied four to eight times. He also claimed, in sharp contrast to the situation at hand, that "the economic problem is not— if we look into the future—the permanent problem of the human race."

Read today, the piece betrays its age and in some of its paragraphs suffers from the prejudices of his time. But it is full of interesting ideas and, in my opinion, hits the key target. Indeed, it exhibits an attitude that over the years has increasingly become a feature of economic thinking: optimism or, if you will, cautious optimism.

The work of economists has not always been perceived thus. Remember the characterization in the mid-nineteenth century by Victorian historian Thomas Carlyle of the economic science of his time as the "dismal science," a reaction to the perception, indebted to Malthus, that permanent poverty is the "natural" equilibrium to which, driven by demographic adjustments, all economies inevitably tend. In fact, the discipline of economics has always had two souls. For one, economics is a science of limits, a discipline that tells us that nothing is free, where proactive exercises in search of immediate results are doomed to fail. The other tells us that the boundaries are dynamic—that time, effort, and good work guarantee that in the long term, limits recede incessantly. Today this second soul is very much alive. Economics is no longer a dismal science. As such, and somewhat presumptuously, in this chapter I will do an exercise in contained optimism of the same nature as Keynes did, but definitely not one of idealization.

But I must take care. I have in mind the anecdote of an important mathematician in a world congress who wanted to imitate the great David Hilbert, who previously had presented at the World Congress of Mathematics in 1900 a set of key problems for the twentieth century. All of them proved to be very difficult, and some are still not yet solved. But the problems that our mathematician presented were all resolved within a year. So I will ask you to be patient and not to judge this chapter as early as I am doing. I plead for the 100 years. I should also warn you that my optimism will be more measured than that of Keynes in some important respects.

First, I review the future of the problems that distressed Keynes. I call these problems the "classic challenges." Then I consider challenges and problems that we now feel much more strongly about than back in 1930. I will not be able to resist the temptation to speculate a little, or rather to extrapolate with certain recklessness on some of the emerging trends in the organization of our economies. From there, I will get straight to wondering what will become of the economic problem in society in the future and what role economists will play in it.

The Future of the Classic Challenges

The main challenge, according to Keynes, was that of living standards, that is, wealth and poverty. Keynes was an optimist, but he was not naive. He was well aware that beyond the rhetoric of the 100 years, the pace of progress would depend on certain conditions. He listed three: the ability to contain population growth, the confidence in scientific advancement, and the ability to avoid wars and civil conflicts. He also mentioned the need for a good rate of capital accumulation and observed that given the above three conditions, this condition would follow. About wars and civil conflicts, I will devote a sentence or two later. The other two conditions are being fulfilled today. Population growth continues, certainly far beyond what Keynes would have wished, but its containment, perhaps even its reversal, is within sight.[2] We are approaching the day when we will finally be cured of the curse of Malthus. Meanwhile, the scientific progress we have experienced in recent decades is nothing short of spectacular, and the promise of future scientific growth is extraordinary.

On this basis and with regard to the classic challenges, I think that there is every reason for optimism, at least if you grant me a new horizon with 100 additional years. In this regard, it should be noted that the challenges are not simply about the standards of living in advanced countries. Here Keynes's predictions are on track to be met generously by 2030, with no need for an extension. But back in 1930 and at the beginning of a depression, Keynes was probably not ambitious enough. Had he been so, I think he would have adopted a more global perspective to include the then less advanced countries, and he would have also recognized that this approach required a longer horizon, say, about 200 years. I think that in that more generous horizon, he would have understood without difficulty and expressed agreement with the following three points:

1. One hundred years from today (around 2113), we will have managed, due to the combination of natural growth and deliberate action, to completely eliminate poverty in the world. By this, I mean that the entire world's population will enjoy a standard of living that in all material respects shall be at least a quarter of what today the inhabitants of richer countries have. In other words, the average citizen of a country that today has a per capita income of $350 (this is roughly the case of Ethiopia) will have in 2113 a life comparable to that of a low-income American citizen today (at constant prices, it would be enough to have an average growth of income per capita about 3.5 percent annually). Of course, we must hope that the goal of eliminating poverty will be achieved long before that. I dare not, however, make predictions about "relative poverty." Obviously, if in the term *relative poverty* we put all the emphasis on the word *relative,* we would expect that this would be a permanent phenomenon.

2. Life expectancy will increase, and in general, our health will be better. This will not come automatically as a consequence of, say, physical exercise, good diet, good public hygiene, and good habits (e.g., not smoking). It will be the consequence of preventive and curative pharmacology and, more generally, the progress of medicine. It seems likely that we will see an increase in the proportion of gross domestic product (GDP) that we spend on health care and fighting the condition that even the most fortunate will

suffer: aging. Here, there is yet much to be done. I fear that in a future more distant than 100 years, the days when life was "nasty, brutish and short" will include our own (as it includes now, at least it is my perception, those of Hobbes).[3] It has been said many times that the twenty-first century will be the century of biomedicine. It is expected that the cost of many medical treatments will decrease dramatically. If the price falls, demand will rise. This in itself will not necessarily increase spending. But it will if a significant cost reduction corresponds to a cost shift from infinity (treatment is impossible) to a finite cost (treatment is possible). We do not consume treatments now whose effect is, say, to make life five years longer for sure. Such treatments simply do not exist. But suppose that these treatments appear on the market tomorrow. Ask yourself what fraction of personal wealth the average citizen would be willing to pay to have access to it.[4]

3. The most advanced countries (those more "progressive") will be, on average, richer. It would not be implausible to repeat during the next 100 years Keynes's prediction for the previous 100 years: properly measured (the components that economists call "hedonic" will be essential in this measurement), we will double our standard of living at least two times.[5]

The New Challenges

Some of the most important worries that concern humanity today would quite possibly have been very surprising to Keynes. Concerns about the limits imposed by the availability of natural resources, the finiteness of the earth, or the desire to preserve the integrity of the air or the diversity of plant and animal life was alien to the central debates of the early decades of the twentieth century. I mean here what we might call "existential concerns," not the permanent and natural concern about the availability of raw materials.

I am convinced that as long as we do not commit gross mistakes in the global governance system, the new challenges, undoubtedly quite real, will not change the cautiously optimistic diagnosis that I have expressed at the conclusion of the review of the classic challenges. Let me elaborate on two specific instances:

1. Because the sun is still in its place, we have an inexhaustible energy source. I do not think in the next 100 years we will find a miraculous solution to the problem of how to put it to work at our convenience, where by

"miraculous," I mean "cheap." The possibility of far-reaching scientific and technological developments in the field of solar energy and others is not to be dismissed, and if we invest adequately in R&D, there will be some.[6] Most likely, therefore, the twenty-first century will be one of expensive, but not prohibitively expensive, energy. And this does not have to induce catastrophes. We do not know if in the long run, the elasticity of substitution will cooperate with us to the point of being greater than unity. It is likely that this will not be the case, so we must be prepared to spend relatively more on energy and relatively less on other things. But there are also many things that have come down and will keep going down in cost. In any case, it is certain that in the long term and for a given date, we will be below the levels of income and welfare that we would reach if energy was cheap, but it is reasonable to assume that we will not be far below and that, in any case, growth will continue being possible. What we must do is to let prices do their work: if the price of energy must increase (because its direct marginal cost is greater or because of corrective taxation for negative externalities), the best thing that can happen is that the price indeed increases. This will induce substitution and will constitute more generally the signal to drive appropriate rearrangements of the economy (e.g., work more from home, make cities adaptable to the bike). In fact, such effects have been felt since the first oil shock in 1973.

2. With respect to the environment, we should refine our thinking and admit that the perimeter relevant to the discussion is not one but many. At one extreme, we have a multitude of local environments around our homes, schools, and workplaces; in the other, we have the earth as a whole, subject to global atmospheric and marine impacts. Bearing this in mind, I reach conclusions about the environment that are similar to those indicated earlier for energy. On the one hand, an increase in how much it is appreciated (driven largely by wealth effects and income elasticities greater than one), and on the other, the imputation of its correct usage prices, transmitted by markets or by regulation, will lead us to devote more resources to its conservation, in a manner that will lead our descendants to think that in this regard, they are better off than we are now.

Although I express optimism here, this optimism is partly a matter of conviction and partly simply a rhetorical resource. It is the former to the extent that if done right, a good result is possible, and it is the latter to the extent that it is implicitly a statement of trust in good work. This trust, I should add, can be especially problematic in situations like climate change, where the current failures in global governance are acute. We should not be at all inhibited in demanding from the international political community a high level of multilateral coordination.[7]

Finally, an aspect of prime importance for this discussion is the pace of change. A full cost–benefit analysis of the adjustment to new technologies of energy production and use should include the costs of transition. One of the most interesting lessons of some branches of modern economic analysis (specifically, behavioral economics[8]) has been to highlight the enormous adaptability of human beings.[9] If, as is legitimate to envisage, changes in the physical environment and, net of short-term volatility, in the market environment are not sharp, then the adjustment process may be gradual and spaced in time, hence relatively not too costly in terms of economic welfare. If from today to tomorrow, a new situation would make the use of cars extremely expensive, the disruption would be great. But if the same effect occurs gradually over several decades, we will adapt to the new situation in a natural and almost imperceptible manner. Transition costs accordingly can be quite limited.

The Organization of the Economy

While I recognize that it is rather pretentious for me to do so, I would like to convey now some thoughts on the features that can inform the institutional functioning of the economy of my great-grandchildren. My single justification is that Keynes also did it.

I will begin with the evolution of work. I do not expect that our descendants will see many changes in this area in the basic contractual aspect (being paid for a service performed), but I think they will in fundamental aspects of its organization. I note four:

1. The concept of daily, or yearly, work will undergo a drastic transformation in one direction: flexibility, as will the workplace. New communications technologies already offer this possibility, and the convenience of not being tied to rigid schedules is considerable, to say the least. The current boom of the issue of reconciliation of work and family duties that we witness in some countries is a first manifestation of a trend that I venture will be unstoppable. Just as the concept of working time will disintegrate

gradually, so will the rigid division between life in school and life at work. Here too the emerging trends are clear.

2. The distinction between the classic "labor contract" and "service contract" will blur. In the future, there will be, above all, civil servants, on the one hand, and on the other, independent workers who will form a set of dense nodes in a network of contracts (one of the many reasons that the future of lawyering is well secured). The centrality of self-employment will run parallel to a transformation of traditional companies. Judging by the past, I would not dare to anticipate what sort of transformation, in terms of scale and pace, governments and the organization of their administrations might experience. The civil service, I forecast, will survive without essential changes.

3. In his lecture, Keynes suggested that the working day of his grandchildren will evolve toward an ideal of three hours per day, and he expressed concern that worker-citizens were unprepared, because of a lack of training, to use their increased leisure time well. This point does not trouble me. If well-educated crowds prefer to occupy their free time watching twenty-two men fight for a ball in a field, and they enjoy it more than a concert, then I feel it is not my business to entertain negative opinions about it. I am less certain that a workday will actually fall to around three hours, for two reasons:

• The first is that in my opinion, work will become interesting. Routine work, including intellectual routine work, can be automated, and automation is becoming less expensive. This will have consequences, for example, on the structure of compensation. Let me give an example close to my experience. Competition among academic institutions plays an important role in setting academic salaries, much more than the reservation price derived from the possibility of alternative employment. I think, and I hope this is not immodesty, that academics are perfectly capable of doing other things but choose not to because they find academic work interesting and satisfactory (they get what a former governor of California called "psychic income"). Hence, the sad consequence is that either competition between academic institutions works or our wages will not improve much.

• The second reason is that the role of career development and, in this context, the motivation from, again, incentives for promotion or just "success," will not diminish, but on the contrary, will continue to be powerful. Incentives, of course, tend to induce effort and working hours. And to the extent that the distinction between the classic worker and an entrepreneur fades, this effort-inducing aspect will gain prominence.

Keynes, let us grant this, could still rescue his conclusion in two ways. The first would take up from the reality that the characteristics of citizens are varied. The stimulatory effect of incentives could manifest itself in only a minority of workers. A majority may still prefer leisure over work so that even if the work is interesting, in the aggregate we may see a decrease in the amount of hours worked. The second way would put the emphasis in variety along the life cycle. We will live longer, and so it is not unlikely that a typical career path might consist of working with some intensity for, say, thirty years, followed by many years of low-intensity work (or alternative intermediate scenarios where high and low work intensities are mixed). And so, on average, hours worked per day will be low.

4. At the time of our great-grandchildren, the manufacture of material necessities in repetitive, standardized ways will occupy just a small fraction of the workforce. This means that there will be plenty of opportunities for customized goods and services, prized for their quality and singularity, and produced by a highly specialized workforce. I imagine, for example, that our descendants may see a reversal of the Baumol–Bowen effect.[10] Recall that this effect tells us that economic progress puts the performing arts (theater, ballet) and the like in a difficult situation: the average wage of performers increases, but the productivity of a live orchestra or ballet company does not. Consequently, costs soar and output shrinks. I am convinced, however, that, for the reasons described above—routine tasks becoming cheaper and high-quality products becoming more valuable—major art productions, intensive in human dedication, will return.

It is common to refer to the economy around us as the "knowledge economy." This is a good term, but it is so generic and overly used that sooner or later, it will be abandoned. I suggest using instead "the economy of accreditation" as a convenient term to designate the new stage we are entering, one where competency, authority, or credibility needs to be certified. On the one hand, when raw information is abundant, the value added by a label that inspires solid confidence is large. On the other hand, and increasingly so, products of all types do not show their most important features at first glance. This is as it should be: the efficiency frontier in the allocation of resources could not be achieved without products of this nature (which may be of a physical nature, such as a mobile phone, or not, such as many financial products). Hence, the growing need is for accreditation in modern economies.

Which mechanisms dispose our economies toward providing accreditation?

Note that the supply of accreditation can be combined with the product itself (the role of brands, for example, can be seen in this light) or can come from a third party. In turn, those involved in accreditation activities may be enterprises, private nonprofit entities, public agencies, universities, media, and even academies. The pertinent question is, however, the usual one: Will the appropriate forms and levels of accreditation occur?

It should be clear after the financial storm that has plagued us in the last few years that massive failures are possible. We are learning the hard way that accreditation is essential for the proper functioning of financial markets and that something has failed in its provision by the market. It seems to me that there has been a consensus, which has proven unjustified, in believing that the informal mechanism of reputation was enough to generate a universe of good practices. That is, it would not matter, for example, who orders or pays for an opinion on the intrinsic risk of a product, or even whether the seller of a financial product will benefit monetarily from the transaction. In each case, the desire to maintain and boost reputation would prevail above the distorting incentives. Although the force of reputation does exist (i.e., a consultant in part also provides accreditation and therefore is aware of harming his or her reputation if he is not careful or accurate enough), it seems it has been dramatically insufficient. Given the size of this market failure, a gap has been opened that is going to be filled in part by regulation and public (accrediting) action, and in part by the emergence of new forms of accreditation.

I think that one of the directions that this evolution will take will be toward more joint responsibility of the financial risks of a product (financial or otherwise) that is accredited. That is, I believe it is going to become more common that those who make a recommendation will also share some of the risk. However, for nonprofit institutions, it may be different; perhaps reputation will turn out to be sufficient. The most important nonprofit institution of all, the state, deserves separate consideration.

My last observation is on taxation. How will taxation evolve in the 100-year horizon we are considering? Maybe not much, since laws have enormous inertia. Nevertheless, I believe that the Tiebout effects will

increasingly be felt at a global scale.[11] Consequently, I do not expect to
see any trend toward convergence in the structure of public goods. The
increase in mobility will tend to reinforce the consequences of the natural diversity of human preferences. However, there are some aspects of
the tax structure, such as corporate taxation, where it seems reasonable
to expect some change. I also anticipate a weakening of a somewhat ata-
vistic feature: that taxation operates on an annual cycle. Either because of
a greater prevalence on consumption or because of a greater prevalence
of linear taxation mechanisms, the effects of the calendar year should be
mitigated.

Is There Something beyond the Economic Problem?

Will the economic problem cease to be "the permanent problem of the
human race" as Keynes asserted it would? I think Keynes got it right. Yet
the economic problem will not disappear entirely, so there will be some
work left for economists.

The economic problem will move from being "the" problem to being
"a" problem. Here I consider myself cautiously optimistic, as Keynes was.
As the level of welfare increases, there will be other problems, some new,
others old, that citizens of the world will consider to be at least as important
as the classic economic problem. But beyond this, I am more pessimistic
than the master. Keynes hoped for a world, perhaps as a sort of poetic flight
into the sky of utopia, in which, freed from slavery to ensure their daily
survival, humans could concentrate on the high tasks of spirit and culture.
He predicted that it would be in this area where we would place our main
concerns in the future. I wish this was the case, but I do not see evidence
in history indicating that this is likely to happen. I do not rule it out, and
in fact I regard it as more likely that the major challenges of the coming
decades and centuries will be problems, profound, disturbing, and even
cruel, that are not among those traditionally considered economic. Can we
be certain that the human race will overcome forever its propensity to war?
How can we know that new challenges and difficult dilemmas, perhaps
arising from the accumulation of wealth or from new technological possibilities, will not appear?

Let us focus for a moment on biology. It is hard not to note that
among the great disasters that have affected humanity and have not been

intentionally caused by humans (i.e., excluding wars and social conflicts), the biological ones figure prominently; among them are the Black Death, the depopulation of the Americas from 1492, and the 1918 flu epidemic.[12] There is a clear trend toward better health, particularly toward an increase in life expectancy, but trends are, after all, random variables and have some variance. It seems to me that we neither dominate nor are we going to dominate during the next century all the biological variables well enough to allow us to say with 100 percent probability that we will not have any new biological disasters.

And there is more, since the biological is not simply one more piece of our environment. We also intervene. And so, in my opinion, issues related to the possibility of genetic selection and breeding in living beings, especially in humans, will be among the more difficult problems we may have to face, not just from the technological and economic perspectives but primarily from the legal and moral viewpoints.

To appreciate how difficult and complex the new problems can get, let me draw attention to an implication, perhaps unlikely but not impossible, of this complexity. A biologically "dichotomized" society is highly undesirable, and we all trust that a responsible society will endeavor to avoid it (though note that today, and without deliberate intervention on selection, health already depends on a variety of socioeconomic characteristics). But what if all of the following three circumstances take place: the state of technology allows the dichotomization, the administrative control of the application of the technology is not feasible, and the technology is expensive, that is, in the aggregate we are not rich enough to guarantee everyone a generous application of its benefits? Would not this represent a resurgence of the economic problem? I understand that it would at two levels: we would have an objective problem of scarcity and a problem of the radical unacceptability of the result of laissez faire. Add to this that all needs are not absolute; there are also relative needs: those arising from the comparison with others. We can agree to dismiss some of these needs as trivial (we would all wish to be brilliant poets), but we should not generalize. It could be that at the time of our grandchildren, some of these relative needs will be felt as fundamental. And, again, to the extent that the cost of eliminating these needs would be high, a form of the economic problem will persist, possibly acutely. In short, and to conclude, I am much less optimistic about the issues just discussed than about the classic and new challenges that I covered before. To put it somewhat bluntly, if humanity in the next 200 years is going to go through a difficult or critical time, I fear it will more likely have a biological or social (wars and conflicts) origin than environmental, energy, or traditional economic.

And what will become of economists? Back in 1930, Keynes's very celebrated position was that in the future (not far from today), "the economic problem . . . should be a matter for specialists—like dentistry. If economists could manage to get themselves thought of as humble, competent people, on a level with dentists, that would be splendid." I leave aside the obvious aristocratic overtones of this judgment (I do not think that Keynes pretended to be merely "modest and competent"—he is confessing that he would not recommend a brilliant grandchild of his own to become an economist). Having dentists in my family, I must say that I do not share Keynes's vision about the profession. But, of course, Keynes used the analogy, unjust toward dentistry, figuratively. What he really meant is that in his view, the discipline of economics will become routine and work mainly through standardized protocols.

I think Keynes erred again on the side of optimism. The economy of the future will be enormously complex (it is already so today) in both its real and financial aspects. But the economy is not static (or, in more technical terms, stationary). Certainly its proper functioning in normal situations will require well-trained dentists. And it will be these experts who will be largely responsible for the economic problem not to be seen as the main problem. The economy will benefit from the quality of their work. Nonetheless, that reality will be punctuated by events and moments of abnormality. In fact, we are now in the middle of one of these episodes. The consequence is that economics as an academic discipline will never be complete. We will not get to know everything because everything changes with the evolution and expansion of economies, and does so in no minor way. It follows that in addition to the normal professional economists, we will need researchers intellectually capable of coping with new phenomena. For example, each macroeconomic crisis moves us toward renewed reflections and economic policy innovations that will be useful and effective to control future crises of a similar type. Lessons are learned. Ben Bernanke, the chairman of the U.S. Federal Reserve, said at a dinner tribute to Milton Friedman on the occasion of his ninetieth birthday, and in reference to his book *Monetary History of the U.S.*, coauthored with Anna Schwartz, "I would like to say to

Milton and Anna, regarding the Great Depression: You are right, we did it. We're very sorry, but thanks to you we will not do it again."[13]

However, sooner or later a new "epidemic" will appear—sorry; I mean a new "crisis"—original and incubated in the folds of the new phenomena of economic life. Because it will be new, it will have no precedent. Typically the analysis will be initially dominated by old perspectives, and you will see deployed the familiar tendency not to recognize how different it is. It could not be otherwise. And while there will always be a previously published article, little known (yet in a leading journal) and with few citations, that anticipated this crisis, it will take a while until the restlessness and the struggle to understand will push our profession toward redoubling its effort of analysis to finally succeed in incorporating anomalies and the unexpected in new and more satisfactory paradigms of normality.

You will have noticed that I used the word *epidemic* instead of *crisis*. Going back to Keynes, and no offense to dentists, this is probably because the best analogy for the future of the economist is that of a physician in both its clinical and in its basic and translational research versions.

Acknowledgments

This chapter is an extended fragment of the induction speech of the same title given at the Real Academia de Ciencias Morales y Políticas in Madrid on March 10, 2009. I am most thankful to Ignacio Palacios-Huerta for thinking it could belong in this book, and also to him and Oscar Volij for arranging the translation.

6 American Politics and Global Progress in the Twenty-First Century

John E. Roemer

As an American, I naturally tend to focus on how developments in my country will affect the world during the next century. At this time, I believe that the most important unknown is politics, not economics. In particular, since the defeat of the Republican Party in the 2008 presidential election and the advent of the first black American president, we have seen the Republican Party move sharply to the right, contrary to what one would have expected a conservative party to do after a defeat by a party to its left. The policies advocated by the Republican Party today, if implemented, would be disastrous not only for the majority of Americans but for the rest of the world. Even after the Democratic victory in November 2012, it is uncertain whether the necessary progress can be made internally to change the American trajectory.[1] I believe the main global problem that must be addressed is the emission of greenhouse gases (GHG), with the consequent effects on global temperature and climate.

The U.S. Congress and president have failed to take any initiative on curbing GHG emissions, and I think this is preventing meaningful global progress on controlling climate change. If the world fails to act and curb emissions strongly in the next fifty years, there is a substantial probability of grave consequences with respect to sea level rises, food production, and mass migrations, both within and between countries. I need not rehearse the possible scenarios here. The Republican Party, most of whose prominent members maintain that global warming is either not occurring or, if it is, is not due to man-made GHG emissions, is misleading the citizenry. My own view is that the United States is the key player in the sense that China would agree to curb emissions if the United States were willing to as well.

From an economic point of view, the problem is solvable without major disruptions in living standards (indeed, even economic growth is possible), but significant government intervention, in the form of taxes and subsidies, and redistribution to protect those who would be hurt by sharp increases in (for example) taxes on fossil fuels would be necessary. (More on this below.) Indeed, I believe there are two sources of the Republican denial with respect to climate change: first, the link between the Republican Party and big business, in particular, the petroleum industry, which wants to continue to profit by exploiting fossil fuels, and second, the understanding that dealing properly with climate change would require substantial state involvement in markets, which Republicans are loath to support.

It is so obviously collectively rational for global society to treat the threat of large increases in temperature seriously that the procrastination exhibited in taking the necessary steps is difficult to fathom. One explanation of that procrastination is that it is difficult for many who do not follow the scientific discussion to understand the problem because of the delay in effects of increasing atmospheric carbon concentration. The various extreme weather events that have occurred in the past decade are probably due to accumulations of carbon in the atmosphere that occurred decades ago, and the effects of the atmospheric carbon concentration—with respect, for example, to melting of ice sheets in Greenland and Antarctica and consequent sea-level rise—will not be fully felt even by the end of this century. In the United States, only a minority of citizens believes that science has the answer (to anything), and this skepticism, along with cognitive dissonance, has made it relatively easy for the Republican Party to prevent any meaningful legislation to address GHG emissions. One can only hope that the defeat of the Republican Party in November 2012, along with a continued increase in extreme weather events which will almost surely occur, will convince Americans that action must be taken, forcing the Republican Party to abandon its opportunistic and ignorant approach to the problem.[2] The second major impediment that the Republican Party is placing with regard to economic progress over the next 100 years is its reluctance to endorse the need to invest in national infrastructure and, in particular, education. Until 1970, each generation in the United States enjoyed a higher secondary school graduation rate than its parents, but this progress came to halt in 1970, with the graduation rate peaking at approximately 80 percent and then declining to around 76 percent.[3] The United States ranks first among countries in the fraction of those fifty-four to sixty-four years old who graduated from high school but eleventh in the fraction of those twenty-five to thirty-four years old who have completed high school. In 2008, it ranked twenty-fifth out of thirty member countries of the Organization for Economic Cooperation and Development in mathematical literacy and twenty-first out of thirty in scientific literacy. The wage gaps between high school dropouts and graduates and between graduates and those with tertiary education have grown substantially, and the failure of the United States to improve its secondary school graduation rate contributes to the creation of a growing class of poor workers. Prominent among these are minorities: the difference in graduation rates between whites, on the one hand, and black and Hispanic students, on the other, has remained fairly constant at around 20 to 25 percent. Barely over half of black and Hispanic students complete high school.

What will be the consequences of this educational failure? A substantial fraction of American workers will grow poorer, both relative to skilled Americans and workers in other countries. American income inequality, which is the highest among the advanced countries and has reached levels not seen since before World War I, will continue to grow.[4] This will increase social polarization in the United States and politically could provide the base for a protectionist movement that would hurt other countries, especially developing ones, whose exports to the United States are increasing or high. It could also provide the political base for xenophobia, producing American behavior that is generally uncooperative, not to say belligerent, on the global stage.

I do not want to imply that if the Democratic party continues to win elections, the situation will be rosy. Given the usual condition of divided government in the United States, it will be difficult to raise the revenue to address infrastructural and educational deficits without the cooperation of a fraction of the opposition party, and with the current state of political polarization, that is not forthcoming. Let me be clear: I believe the political polarization reflects citizen opinion, which is strongly influenced by political leadership, and, indeed, by the plethora of right-wing think tanks that formed, predominantly in the 1970s, to spread the laissez-faire, antistate gospel.

In the past forty years, the main agents of progressive political education of the American working class, the trade unions, have virtually disappeared. In 2010, union density fell to its lowest rate in 70 years (11.9 percent), while that figure among private sector workers fell to its lowest rate in a century (6.9 percent). The high point, in the 1950s, was 35 percent. This cannot be a consequence solely of changes in the sectoral composition of employment, because Canadian union density declined only slightly over this period, remaining above 30 percent. The decline in union power in the United States is due to a protracted attack on unions and their organizers by firms, probably given a big boost by Ronald Reagan's firing of eleven thousand unionized air traffic controllers in 1981 during a strike, leading to the decertification of their union, PATCO.

Although American trade unions were not, for the most part, left wing (the CIO played its antileft part during the McCarthy period by expelling ten unions with Communist or left-wing leadership), they provided some solidaristic ideology that equipped workers with the mental tools necessary to defend themselves against exploitation. Absent the unions and union ideology, firms have been able to hold the increase in real wages for many categories of workers substantially below the increase in labor productivity. The largest private employer in the world, Walmart, provides an illustration. Walmart fights attempts at union organization viciously and pays low salaries and minimal benefits while teaching its workers how to augment their income by applying for government income support. In 2011, corporate profits in the United States reached their highest share in national income since 1950, at 12.6 percent, while labor's share fell to its smallest since 1955, at 54.9 percent. Labor's share before 2000 averaged 64 percent.

It is difficult to predict what the political consequences of this increasing economic polarization in the United States will be and what will be their knock-on effects for the rest of the world. For the first time in over a century, a substantial fraction of the population—those with at most a secondary level of education—will be worse off than their parents, certainly relative to those with tertiary education and perhaps even in absolute terms. From what source could the leadership emerge to equip those who are losing with the political and economic organization to reverse this trend?

Certainly not the Democratic party, which will only reflect what voters believe. Indeed, the deregulation that contributed to the financial crisis of 2008 occurred during the administration of Bill Clinton. As long as a large number of voters are convinced that government is inefficient and taxes should not be increased—ideas that right-wing think tanks have carefully nurtured among the citizenry during the past forty years—the Democratic party will be powerless to effect the necessary changes.

What caused perhaps the most progressive development in the past 100 years: the growth of welfare states in the advanced countries? I think the important events were the Great Depression and World War II. The war was important in two ways: first, solidaristic ideology increased among citizens of western Europe and the United States in the fight against fascism, and second, in western Europe (but not the United States), the war wiped out a great deal of wealth, creating a large constituency for social insurance. In the first postwar elections, the left (socialist and Communist parties) won approximately half the vote in every democratic European country. Let me comment on the second cause just enumerated. It is difficult to pass universal social insurance legislation if citizens face very different economic risks: any simple insurance plan (where each contributes a given fraction of his or her income as a premium and receives a given fraction of his or her income when he or she is unemployed or ill) will require that low-risk groups subsidize high-risk groups. By wiping out substantial amounts of wealth in Europe, World War II homogenized risks among the citizenries, thus reducing the actuarial unfairness of universal insurance. I conjecture this was an important cause of the massive voter approval and consequent growth of the European welfare states.

After experiencing the beneficent results of social insurance, I believe that citizen preferences changed, to become more equality loving. Thus, the right-wing antitax, antistate ideology that has made such progress in the United States has remained marginal in Europe. The main challenge that Europe has faced, and continues to face, is to incorporate relatively poor immigrants into its economy and society. This has reduced the support for the welfare state among a fraction of the citizenry, as seen by the growth in some countries of xenophobic, right-wing parties, such as the Front National in France. I think, however, that Europe will succeed in incorporating immigrants without the dissolution of its welfare states: thus far, it has.

Some readers will protest that the greatest challenge facing Europe is the present crisis of the eurozone engendered by the financial crisis of 2008. I do not believe that this is a crisis for the welfare state as such, although undoubtedly some entitlements will be reduced in the southern European countries (Greece, Italy, Spain, Portugal) in the short or medium term. Adopting a common currency was a progressive development and, I believe, has substantially increased the welfare of Europeans, especially in the poorer southern countries. But northern Europeans, in particular

Germans, have also profited from the monetary union. (Germany had the foresight to hold down unit labor cost increases, while other countries did not, enabling it to profit greatly in the export market.) Granted, the design was not perfect, especially with regard to the lack of fiscal union. Except for Greece, whose politicians evidently exploited the opportunities for EU subsidies and failed to address corruption (in the form of tax evasion and political payoffs to state workers), modernize the economy, and hold down unit labor costs, the problems are mainly due to the real estate bubble prior to 2008. As such, it is the limited solidarity that the citizens of the northern rich countries feel toward the citizens of southern poor ones that prevents a resolution of the euro crisis. I believe it is likely that economic rationality will prevail, in the sense that Germans and northern Europeans will understand—what I believe to be true—that maintaining the eurozone is in their interest, as well as the interest of the southern Europeans, and they will implement transfers that will enable the South to overcome the crisis. The failure to continue to develop a federal European structure would be unfortunate for all Europeans. But it would also be terribly unfortunate for the world because Europe presents the best example of egalitarian economic institutions. To the extent that it remains a successful economic power and provides well for its citizens, it will influence the developing world to adopt those institutions.

Perhaps the most hopeful and exciting economic development of the past thirty years has been the amazing economic development of China and, more recently, the rapid economic development in Brazil, India, and some other poor countries. It seems that the twenty-first century will be the one where a significant fraction of the global poor will rise to approximately the economic level of the rich countries. Of course, this will entail a redistribution of global political power. After the dissolution of the Soviet state in 1991, the United States enjoyed unparalleled global influence for a brief period. This will not last, and one of the important uncertainties is how the United States will handle its decreasing global hegemony. I have argued that the healthiest prospect for the world would be that the United States repair its internal infrastructural and educational deficits so that it does not suffer too rapid a relative decrease in its economic position, and hence does not become a global belligerent.

Some might object that I have too positive an evaluation of the possibilities for the economic convergence of China, India, and Brazil (perhaps others) with the current advanced countries of the global North. It is doubt-less true that the rapid growth rates in these countries are in large part due to low labor costs, the urbanization and proletarianization of the peasantry, and the imitation of technologies that have been invented in the North. As labor costs rise due to increases in capital-labor ratios and education and these countries approach the technological frontier, growth will slow, and perhaps the superiority of the United States in research and tertiary education will keep it at the technological frontier, enabling it to remain the most advanced economy in the world. The United States holds the vast plurality of Nobel prizes; it may take considerable time for the rapidly grow-ing developing countries to create research institutions that will enable it to challenge the United States on this dimension. If this turns out to be the case, I would be wrong to predict that the United States will, in the com-ing century, become less globally powerful than some other country (like China), although I do insist that its relative influence will decline.

A further critique of my prediction of convergence, especially with regard to China, can be raised because of China's internal political fragil-ity. I believe that political dictatorship cannot last for too many more years or decades if China continues to develop economically. Indeed, corrup-tion is pervasive and visible in China, perhaps most clearly illustrated by the continuing insistence that the Chinese Communist party is "self-less," while the children of party leaders (the "princelings") are virtually all mul-timillionaires due to their family connections. How China will handle the transition to democracy is a huge unknown and will have important conse-quences for the rest of the world. The most hopeful scenario is that politi-cal competition develops gradually in China, within the existing political institutions, especially within the Communist party, and that from this emerges a structure of independent political parties and democratic politi-cal competition. But the transition to democracy may not be so pacific. In contrast, Brazil and India have already successfully managed the demo-cratic transition.

Keynes, in the essay that inspired this book, did not envision World War II, the development of the European welfare states, or the rapid economic growth of a substantial portion of the poor world. (In fact, he limited the purview of his comments to what he called the "progressive," meaning the advanced, economies.) He predicted a growth in income per capita in the advanced countries of between four- and eightfold, and this concomitant with a reduction of the workweek to fifteen hours. In Europe, the number of days in the work year has declined substantially over the past eighty years. Germans today work an average of fourteen hundred hours per year: for a fifty-week year, probably the norm when Keynes was writing, this translates to an average of twenty-eight hours per week. Germany is near the top of the list in the number of annual hours of leisure. Thus, given the actual reduction in the workweek that has occurred, roughly to twice as many hours as he predicted, Keynes would have conjectured an increase in income per capita of between eight- and sixteen-fold (holding constant his implicit view on the increase in productivity).

If real growth per capita in the advanced countries has been approximately 2 percent annually, then in a century, per capita incomes would increase about sevenfold—so Keynes, it appears, was too optimistic about productivity growth, as well as too optimistic about decreases in the length of the working year. With regard to the latter, he underestimated the power of advertising in stimulating demand for an ever-increasing living standard among the middle and rich classes, and he perhaps also underestimated the degree to which income-class differences would remain due to immigration and the only partial success of educational systems in eliminating skill and wage differentials.

I believe the remarkable achievement of the advanced economies during the twentieth century was their progress toward equalizing the distribution of income. What worries me most about recent developments is the regression on this dimension, especially in the United States, but to an extent in some European countries as well (particularly the United States). This reduction in inequality has been achieved along with average real income growth of approximately 2 percent annually.

But if we are to deal successfully with climate change, I think that average income growth in the advanced countries will have to be limited to about 1 percent annually over the next century, and I am unsure what effect such a slowdown would have on inequality. Let me elaborate. A global reduction of GHG emissions to a level that would maintain atmospheric carbon concentrations at no more than 450 parts per million (ppm) during the next century can be accomplished only with an agreement between the two largest emitters, the United States and China, to reduce their emissions substantially. (Many argue that 450 ppm is too high for safety, so this is a conservative condition.) Llavador, Roemer, and Silvestre argue that reaching such a negotiated global agreement to restrict emissions requires that the date at which the United States and China would have converged in income per capita under business as usual, and absent the climate change problem, not be affected by the necessary reductions in emissions.[5] They take that conditional convergence as occurring in seventy-five years for China and the United States and ask how a world composed of a South that looks like China and a North that looks like the United States (in terms of economic endowments and population) could converge in seventy-five years, restricting global emissions to a path on which atmospheric carbon concentration converges to 450 ppm. The authors compute that there is a path of resource allocation, including the allocation of emissions over the period to the global North and South, on which convergence in welfare per capita occurs if the North's real welfare per capita growth rate is maintained constantly at 1 percent annually. But such convergence is not possible, given the global emissions restriction, if the annual northern growth rate is significantly higher than 1 percent.

Thus, Llavador, Silvestre, and I believe that meeting the climate change challenge requires negotiating a deal that does not delay the growth factor of the global South relative to the global North, which in turn is consistent with a northern welfare growth rate capped at around 1 percent annually in real terms. Even this estimate is optimistic, given what I have noted about U.S. politics, because our optimization assumes that technological innovation and human capital increase at rates that are feasible based on historical estimates. The calculation puts no political constraint on whether the North will make the necessary infrastructural and educational investments to implement the optimal path.

Thus, I believe that average growth in the North must be limited to 1 percent annually in real terms in order to meet the climate change challenge, and this is so on the optimal path of resource allocation, which assumes no political constraints internal to each region. Were such a path to be implemented, the growth rate of the pie in the North would be substantially smaller than it has been over the past century, and this raises the question of whether reductions in inequality are politically feasible because the reductions would entail a substantially smaller growth rate for the wealthiest households.

It is difficult to imagine a political realignment occurring that would render this path politically feasible in the United States given its recent history. Certainly if the ideology of the Republican party continues to attract approximately one-half the U.S. population, meeting the climate change challenge will be impossible. What could engender a more rational reaction to the challenges of the coming century among American voters? Probably only an economic crisis, brought on by an untamed financial sector, that is considerably more destructive than the 2008 crisis. Despite the severity of the recent crisis, its effect on citizens was much less than that of the Great Depression; perhaps that magnitude of unemployment and wealth destruction will be necessary to jolt Americans out of the laissez-faire and individualistic ideology that has taken hold in the past forty years. Of course, one cannot wish for such a catastrophe, but without one, can there be hope for change in the American political trajectory? Given the unwillingness of either political party in the United States to break up the big banks and investment houses and to separate investment from the traditional banking functions of these firms, another crisis is likely to occur. The only more pacific transitions to a more sustainable trajectory in the United States that I can imagine might be effected by changing demography and, in particular, the growth of the Hispanic vote or the calculation by the Republican party that it must move toward the center and change its hyper-antistatist policies to remain a political player.

7   In 100 Years

Alvin E. Roth

For those of you reading this chapter in 2113, let me introduce myself by saying that in the late twentieth and and early twenty-first centuries, I studied the design of matching markets: those in which price alone does not clear the market and so participants cannot just choose what they want (even if they can afford it); they also have to be chosen. These are markets that involve application or selection processes or other forms of courtship. Matching markets determine some of the most important events of our lives: where we go to school, whom we marry, what jobs we get, even whether we get a lifesaving organ for transplant if we should need one.[1] So I will concentrate my predictions on these things—schools, jobs, marriage and family, and medicine—along with some thoughts about the possible state of economic expertise, that is, the things that economists produce and sell.

Part of my prediction technique will be to think about which aspects of those things may have, in 100 years, become commodities that can be had by anyone who has the price and wants to buy them, and which things will continue to be allocated by matching markets in which each side of the market has to choose and be chosen by their counterparties on the other side.

I have also spent some time studying how some kinds of transactions are regarded as repugnant, in some times and places, and how this constrains what markets we see.[2] By *repugnant transaction,* I mean a transaction that some people would willingly engage in but that others wish to prevent. Over the long sweep of history, some formerly repugnant transactions have come to be regarded as ordinary, while other ordinary transactions have come to be regarded as repugnant, often with important consequences. For example, charging (and paying) interest on loans was regarded as repugnant for centuries, but no longer is for most of the world (although Islamic law still forbids it). It is hard to imagine how the global markets for capital and the economic activity they support would have developed if interest were still repugnant. And markets for slaves that once thrived, for example, are now repugnant. Slavery and other forms of involuntary servitude, including servitude initially entered into voluntarily, like indentured servitude, are now illegal in most of the world. This is notable not least because entering into indentured servitude was once the most common way of purchasing passage across the Atlantic Ocean to America. (Although this is no longer a legal contract, there are still black markets in which illegal immigrants essentially indenture themselves in return for being smuggled into the United States.) So I will try predicting some currently repugnant transactions that may not be repugnant in 2113 and speculate about some transactions we now see that may become repugnant.

There are several ways to go about making predictions, but surprising predictions for 100 years in the future are inevitably little more than guesses, maybe educated guesses. The most reliable prediction method for the short term is to extrapolate current trends, and this may serve for the long term as well, supplemented by guesses at as-yet-unrealized consequences of trends that will be realized as they progress. Somewhat more risky is to guess which current trends will run their course and be only a memory. And guesses about what entirely new developments will emerge are close to science fiction, since the nature of really new developments (e.g., antigravity machines, contact with extraterrestrial intelligence) is that we have little on which to base our guesses. But we can confidently predict that some very unpredictable developments will have an outsized influence in 100 years, just as antibiotics and integrated circuits and the rise and fall of totalitarian ideologies have influenced life in the past 100 years in ways that could not have been predicted in 1913. So I will not attempt to guess at the really unpredictable. Instead, extrapolation will make up the bulk of my predictions, but I also take a stab at predicting that the trend toward devoting an ever larger proportion of resources to medical expenditures will eventually reverse itself, although predictions of that sort do not have a high success rate (e.g., Malthus predicting famine because population growth just could not continue).

To set the stage, I think the biggest trend of future history (if it is not disrupted by environmental catastrophe, or descent into widespread terrorism, or warfare with weapons of mass destruction) is that the world economy will continue to grow and become more connected. Material prosperity will continue to increase, population will grow, and healthy longevity will increase.

While increased prosperity will not eliminate competition, it will give people more choices about whether and how hard to compete. Many will opt to begin on a slower track, spending more time accumulating youthful experience prior to the assumption of a full set of adult responsibilities marked by completion of full-time education, careers, marriage, and children. Retirement will also be a longer part of a productive life, and new forms of retirement will emerge, combining work and leisure and study and philanthropy.

Despite the increase in prosperity, some goods, services, statuses, and knowledge still will be scarce. People who don't wish to settle for the simple life will continue to have incentives to strive and compete. For those who wish to compete, there will be technological developments that enhance competitiveness and allow them to work harder than ever. Some of these, like performance-enhancing drugs, are beginning to be available today but are widely regarded as repugnant. That repugnance seems likely to fade. Other technologies, which we begin to glimpse as possibilities today, like selecting the genetic characteristics of our children, may remain repugnant and illegal but nevertheless become widely available and tempting.

We already see performance-enhancing drugs used in competitive sports, despite being widely banned. But while we may continue to try to cancel sporting victories won with the assistance of drugs, we are unlikely to decline cancer cures or software or theorems produced with the assistance of drugs that aid concentration, memory, or intelligence. Safe performance-enhancing drugs may come to be seen as akin to good nutrition (much as we think children should drink milk) and to fashionable behavior (much the way we like good coffee today). And just as drugs may already not be optional to reach the highest level in some competitive sports, they may not be optional in future competitive careers. When assistant professors of economics in 2113 fall behind their expected production of an article a week, their department chair may suggest that they increase their dose of creativity-enhancing or attention-focusing pharmaceuticals to boost their chance of tenure. And some drugs—memory enhancers, say—may be seen not as performance enhancers but as cures for things we did not previously think of as diseases (much as erectile dysfunction came to be seen as a disease once it could be treated with pharmaceuticals). In 2113 our descendants will have trouble remembering a time when it was hard to remember the names of all the people they met, just as they may find it hard to understand why it was hard to run marathons on two consecutive days.

Similar to the way drugs will allow us to improve our own performance, increased understanding of genetics, reproduction, and fetal development will allow parents to select or manipulate some of the genetic endowment of their children. Some of these options will remain repugnant even as they become more widely available, while others may come to be seen as part of careful child rearing. To the extent that these technologies are subject to legal limitations in some places and not in others, they will help fuel an international market in reproductive technology, as some parents travel to places that will cater to their desire to enhance the abilities of their children. We already see the beginnings of such a market, as access to fertility treatments, and markets for eggs and sperm and surrogate wombs are more available in the United States and India than in many other places, and consequently draw "fertility tourists."

This trend will continue, and various reproductive options will become largely commoditized and separated from sexual intercourse (not to mention traditional heterosexual marriage) and the need to be matched with a biologically appropriate willing coparent. This will, incidentally, help facilitate nontraditional forms of marriage and child rearing, as well as delayed marriage and single parenthood, and many of these alternative arrangements (e.g., same-sex marriage and polygamy) will no longer be regarded with the repugnance and legal barriers that still greet them today in many places, just as many, if not most, forms of consensual sexual relations between adults are no longer today regarded in many places with the repugnance of centuries past.

Despite the commoditization of reproductive services, I expect that families will remain one of the main units of production—certainly of children—and of consumption of all sorts of household goods and comforts. Long-term (even if not lifetime) relationships will remain important as work and play are increasingly globalized, so that personal fixed points become a larger part of people's sense of who they are. But in the other direction, generations will be longer, and child rearing will take up a smaller proportion of longer healthy lifetimes, which may make divorce more common and perhaps lead to new forms of polygamy-over-lifetime relationships to supplement the serial monogamy that sometimes today accompanies high divorce rates.

Not only drugs will enhance performance, but, less controversial, so will increasingly powerful and personal computation. But this will lead to rising concerns about personal data and privacy, and certain kinds of transactions involving personal data that are not yet repugnant may become so. For example, as personal data become increasingly valuable for business purposes, such data may also come to be viewed more like intellectual property, with protections akin to patent and copyright protection today, moderated by fair use exceptions, so that uncompensated use of transactional data may come to seem repugnant, or at least subject to limitations. Already in 2013 there are consensual transactions in personal data (e.g., when supermarket customers are offered compensation in the form of discounts for allowing their identity to be linked to their purchases as their bar code data are collected at the cash register), while uncompensated uses of data generated through various transactions are coming under scrutiny, particularly when there is doubt that appropriate consent can be given.

More important, data may become a civil rights issue. Today my smart phone gives me the Internet in my pocket, but well before 2113, the camera in my contact lens should be able to use face recognition software to search vast databases and display for me a great deal of data about the people I see. This will change the meaning of *search*, perhaps shifting the balance between the word that today indicates what we do with Google, toward the more legal meaning of what police do when they enter your home with a warrant. That is, when I can glance at you and have immediate access to all your available data, guarding those data may become increasingly important. Already today we generate a data stream through our purchases, travel, and encounters with many levels of bureaucracy (from marriage records to police and court cases). Much of this is public, and much more of it is electronically searchable by those with access. Laws defining who has access to what data about individuals under what circumstances will likely become increasingly important, and all kinds of data may be subject to restrictions about its sale or transfer, with some transactions coming to be regarded as repugnant and increasingly regulated, if not prohibited by law. We have already begun to see this beginning with medical records.

Medicine will likely be as different in 2113 from today as today's medicine is from 1913. Some medical and public health advances will be against predictable physical failings—heart attacks and many more cancers will be curable or avoidable, for example. There may also be setbacks: one of our greatest advances of the past 100 years, the development of antibiotics and vaccines, may come to be seen as having reached and receded from a high-water mark. Infectious diseases may have a renaissance as evolution creates drug-resistant bacteria or vaccine-eluding viruses, while increased globalization facilitates the rapid spread of infection around the world. To the extent that infectious diseases remain dangerous, sexually transmitted diseases may, in 2113, have mediated changes in social conventions about love and marriage and further changed some of the trade-offs between sexual fidelity and promiscuity. These changes may be particularly important if they interact with how many children people choose to have.

Some of the big (but hard-to-predict) changes in medicine will be technological. For example, I have worked on developing kidney exchange networks that increase the number of kidney patients who can receive transplant organs from living donors. I bet that by 2113, the whole idea of cutting a kidney out of one person and sewing it into another will seem like an ancient barbarity. But it is hard to guess whether transplantation will have been replaced by xeno-transplantation to give you a working kidney grown in a farm animal, or stem cell therapies to grow healthy new kidneys of your own, or artificial kidneys, or simply better treatment of diseases that now cause kidney failure.

Many of these alternatives may be both longer lasting and cheaper than transplantation. This is what makes me think that while medicine could continue to be an ever growing part of the economy as the population gets older, it also could (sweet thought) become like farming—so efficient that a smaller part of the economy provides all of it that we need. If progress in preventive medicine keeps pace with other advances and we come to spend most of our lives as healthy as twenty year olds and then expire peacefully at home, it could be that doctors, like farmers, will meet our needs as a much smaller industry that mostly produces products out of commodity-like inputs that can be assembled into personalized packages, much as people in the developed world today enjoy a wide variety of year-round agricultural commodities that would have been beyond the reach of all but the very richest people in 1913.

I noted how performance-enhancing drugs may become essential for professors seeking tenure. Of course, tenure may be increasingly concentrated at elite universities, which will remain recognizable by their high tuition together with abundant financial aid to support expensive teaching in residential communities of scholars to which admission is selective. Despite the fact that information itself will be increasingly available elsewhere, elite universities will persist for many of the same reasons that cities will, including not only information transmission but also signaling and networking for various purposes, including matchmaking. High education couples will continue to pair off, but people pursuing high-intensity careers may marry those pursuing lower-intensity careers as mobility and long hours continue to be important in competitive careers. As marriage is delayed, the postgraduation educational network may become more important for this, and perhaps we will see new kinds of matchmaking.

Nevertheless, elite universities and residential campuses will continue to become smaller parts of the education industry. (A related possibility is that the world's fanciest universities will continue to open branch campuses around the world and that this will serve to foster really good distance education with professors in one place lecturing to many students by electronic means, with students able to interact with each other as if they were in one location.) There will be lots more access to information/education on demand, without the logistical constraints of conventional classes and courses. The trend toward more diverse kinds of education will continue. Mass postsecondary education will continue to evolve, perhaps with electronic outsourcing of particular workforce-related kinds of education and training. So those parts of postsecondary education most closely connected to specific job-related skills will likely become more decentralized and commoditized and electronic, even while elite universities remain very recognizable, as universities in 2013 would be quite recognizable to students and professors from 1913, despite big changes, many of which (e.g., computers and electronic communications) are reflections of how those have changed society in general rather than reflections of a change in universities' role in society.

But for those who can gain access to it, several years of study in comfortable surroundings will remain a desirable way of accumulating human capital while preparing for and connecting with the adult world. This may continue to become a social marker that will to some extent supplant socioeconomic status. In the U.S. presidential election of 2008, in which the candidates were Barack Obama and John McCain, the candidate who was a multimillionaire by marriage and the son and grandson of admirals tried with considerable success to cast the graduate of Columbia and Harvard as a representative of the elite.

But teaching and networking are not the only things that go on at universities; they are also the bastion of investigator-initiated basic research. As technology advances, commercial research and development will continue to grow in importance, but universities will remain important for basic research. Here too networks will remain valuable for introducing and validating scholars, even while physical proximity becomes less critical. Already in 1990 I was a coauthor of a paper in which my coauthors did not all know one another, and in 2013 much less of my communication with coauthors is face-to-face than when I began to do research in the 1970s. However, it is still the case that most of my collaborations begin with face-to-face interaction. As the quality and ease of distance communication improve, this may become a quaint antiquity, in which case research collaborations should become ever more common across the boundaries of particular universities and between university-based scholars and those at other kinds of institutions.

This brings me to predictions about the work that economists do. Economics will still be at the vanguard of social science, partly because it will continue to incorporate insights and data that were once seen as sociology and political science, just as it has already begun to assimilate insights from psychology, as well as biology.

Poverty will remain (development will still be a field of economics), but poverty in the developing world 100 years from now may look more like poverty in the developed world today, or perhaps the poor in the developing world will have the material prosperity that the middle class does in the developed world today, especially since many of the markers of what used to be middle-class prosperity will grow cheaper, much as telephones and televisions and computers have already. Consequently, development economics will be more closely integrated with the rest of practical and academic economics than it is today.

One important change in the economy will be in the kinds of marketplaces that will become available. As markets have become more computerized (and as we have started to understand better what well-designed marketplaces do), "smart markets" that do some of the work that market participants formerly had to do have already become possible. For example, bidders in eBay auctions can submit reservation prices to a software proxy agent, and participants in school choice or labor-market clearinghouses can submit preference lists; in each case, the market uses that information on the participant's behalf without requiring further attention. That is, computers have already increasingly become an important part of markets and marketplaces, from the computerized cash registers that also help stores monitor inventory, to the computerized stock exchanges that let trades be executed ever more quickly, to the smart markets that start to verge a little on artificial intelligence, acting as proxies for individual agents and using the information submitted on behalf of agents to compute outcomes that could not have been found in markets run without computers (think combinatorial auctions and stable matching mechanisms).

As computers and computer science continue to advance, artificial intelligence will have crossed the barrier so that some parts of technology will be self-directing—able to operate not merely without direct human supervision but able to formulate intermediate goals as well as plans of action to achieve them. Artificial intelligences may become companions (distant descendants of today's iPhone games), friends, advisors (distant descendants of today's GPS navigation advisors that can sound disappointed when we miss a turn), and market intermediaries. As computer assistance becomes more ubiquitous in all aspects of life, some of that assistance will be in markets, helping us piece together things we need (such as airline, hotel, and rental car reservations for different legs of a multipart journey) the way a skilled assistant would today, without the time-consuming personal attention that some person would have to give to the task. The next step will be to have our proxies help us decide which trips to take (e.g., which seminar and conference invitations to accept) and how to schedule them and structure the journeys involved, while our proxies interact with the scheduling proxies of the seminar and conference organizers. (As suggested above, I am guessing that some seminars and conferences will still involve travel. Although electronic communications will have made travel unnecessary for the seminar presentation itself, the after-seminar dinner and the exchange of ideas it fosters, not to mention the matchmaking among similarly inclined investigators and potential coauthors, may still be better in the flesh.)

Computerized markets will make market design more important, as many market details will have to be embodied in computer code. But many kinds of market design that are today crafted by specialists will have passed from frontier knowledge to whatever is then the equivalent of shrink-wrapped software, much the way that techniques of mathematical optimization that once were the domain of PhDs in operations research have become available in software packages. But there will still be unsolved problems of organization and coordination, so market design (or, more generally, *design economics* dealing not just with markets but with the design of all forms of organizing, transacting, and allocating) will have become and will remain an important part of economics. And some of what economists do will have come to be regarded as engineering. It will not be surprising to anyone in 2113 that questions of, say, how to organize school choice are handled better than they were in 2013, just as it will not be surprising that bridges are lighter and longer, even if some of the underlying economic and physical principles have been well understood for a long time. Other kinds of advances will have produced better ways to apply those principles.

To summarize the predictions I have made here for about 100 years from now, I think that the trend of increasing prosperity will continue, but that it will not necessarily bring us all lives of leisure, as Keynes predicted in 1930.[3] Many people will work harder than ever before, and some of the things some of us will do to work more efficiently, like taking performance-enhancing drugs, will go from being repugnant today to ordinary in the future. Other things we do eagerly today, like use computers for access to more and more data, may become repugnant in some respects as privacy of personal data moves to the forefront of civil rights issues. And while medical advances will continue on all fronts and advances in preventive medicine will make medical care and long-lived good health more widely available, some kinds of medicine, including reproductive medicine along with other aspects of reproduction, will become commoditized, while others, such as genetic manipulation of various sorts, may become repugnant. Some kinds of education will become commoditized, but among the matching markets that we see today, selective admissions to elite universities will remain, as will networking and matchmaking for family formation (under a wider variety of marital forms) and, perhaps increasingly, for research collaborators and other kinds of business partners. And there will still be economists, and economic mysteries to unravel, including those that will arise from the increased computerization of markets and marketplaces. Much of market design that we struggle to understand today will have become commoditized and be found in off-the-shelf software, but understanding how to design novel markets and fix market failures will remain an active concern of our economist grandchildren.

Keynes, in writing about the future of economics, said, "If economists could manage to get themselves thought of as humble, competent people, on a level with dentists, that would be splendid!" Perhaps if we replace *dentists* with *engineers*, that is still a good goal for the next hundred years.

8 The Risks of the Next Century and Their Management

Robert J. Shiller

The next century carries with it any number of risks as an unprecedented number of people attempt to live well on a planet with limited and endangered resources, with ever more dangerous strategic weapons of mass destruction, and with the flourishing of new information technologies that stir up labor markets and create career risks. Much of the management of these risks will be in the domain of science and engineering, but there is also the purely financial and insurance domain, and the subject of this chapter. There is an expectation that with the help of new technology, new and far better risk management will be deployed against all these risks. We can hope, or expect, to see a better kind of risk management that offsets the fears we have for the next century—risk management that can be coupled with incentives for scientists and engineers to develop and implement better solutions to the fundamental problems associated with these risks.

Most of us are not accustomed to thinking about the kinds of risks that can unfold over a century. It is far too easy to be complacent about them. To make these seem real, it is useful to put these risks in a long-term historical perspective. One might consider reading Jared Diamond's *Collapse*, which depicts major economic catastrophes of past centuries, or Charles Mann's *1491*, which presents a picture of a far more advanced and populous America before Columbus than we have been accustomed to imagining, and therefore allowed us to see the magnitude of the collapse of the Native American economy after 1492.[1] One can only imagine what other changes could appear within a hundred years when environmental catastrophes occur, or major wars or epidemics occur, or certain populations gain an extreme economic superiority over others from technological revolutions.

At the same time, the theory of financial risk management has made major advances: the mathematical theory is getting better and better, and the development of behavioral economics is creating possibilities of making financial solutions congenial to real people. There has also been a trend toward the democratization of risk management—toward making risk management principles available to a much higher fraction of the world population. Centuries ago, only the wealthiest and most sophisticated had any insurance or banking services or portfolio services, and now, at least in advanced countries, these are fairly widely disseminated.

But there is much more to do to keep these trends going. Fortunately, new information technology, which is growing at a breathtaking pace, can support this trend, and even accelerate it in the next century.

The trend toward better risk management depends for its continuance on experimentation with new techniques of risk management, and so the outcome of any given experiment is uncertain and can have setbacks. The recent financial crisis, which began with the U.S. subprime crisis in 2007 and continued with the European sovereign debt crisis starting in 2009, is a singular example of such a setback. But as we learn more and more through time about how to handle such crises, the better off we will be.

It is not possible to predict the future well without getting into proposing new ideas for the future. If we are to do more than extrapolate current trends, we have to rely on our sense of what are essentially good ideas for the future, with the faith that genuine good ideas, which may still be unworkable or not widely known today, will be implemented later. Moreover, we then have to take risks fleshing out some of the details of the ideas, so that we can see how they might work, and this may tend to give them an idiosyncratic flair. I will include here some of the proposals in my books, notably *Macro Markets: Creating Institutions for Managing Society's Largest Economic Risks* (1994), *New Financial Order: Risk in the Twenty-First Century* (2003), and *Finance and the Good Society* (2012).[2] For this chapter, which is about predicting the next century, I will try to look especially at the core ideas that I am confident are often also on others' minds and will be more so in the future.

Risk Management in a New World Almost Having Artificial Intelligence

Computer scientists seem to be in near agreement that true artificial intelligence is out of our reach, at least for the next century. There are some, however, who think real artificial intelligence is coming soon.[3] Whether or not true artificial intelligence is developed, most likely the information technology revolution that has dazzled us with repeated innovations will continue to improve so as to offer better opportunities, though the machines will still not understand. It appears that you will still need to have, for example, a real doctor and a real lawyer. But apparently it is to be expected that the machines will come close enough to true intelligence to fool us some of the time and will provide an alternative to human intelligence that we will be using much, or even most, of the time. One's doctor and lawyer will be heavily invested in (if not even physically—inside their brains, as some suggest—connected to) such machines. This immense computing power will both create risks and offer possibilities for risk mitigation.

An important consequence of this approach to artificial intelligence will be a long trend toward unification of global culture. The sociologist Emile Durkheim described society as having a "collective consciousness," and the sociologist Maurice Halbwachs extended this concept to that of "collective memory."[4] If we all remember much the same facts, we have the same evidence to promote our worldviews and will tend to arrive at similar worldviews. Writing in their day, however, they never could have imagined how much stronger these factors would come to be with modern information technology. This will make the world economy perhaps more efficient, but it will also create greater correlations across countries and regions, and hence greater vulnerability to international economic collapse.

In this world with near artificial intelligence, new kinds of subcultures will tend to arise that are no longer defined by geographical coincidence. In particular, there is likely to develop a cosmopolitan culture of the people most connected with artificial intelligence, a sort of world elite, who, by their constant communications, will tend to develop some loyalties to each other rather than to their geographical neighbors, while billions of others will form a worldwide string of ghettos. Even among the elite, the globalization of culture will not be complete, and there will still be ancient national and traditional ethnic and religious rivalries and the potential for war.

There will be no central authority to be in control of all of these processes that create risks for individuals and for larger society. We must approach these risks with all of the new kinds of risk management functions that we can invent.

Big Data Create Big Opportunities to Contain Our Risks

We are already living in an age of big data—of massive data sets shared around the world—and this will be even more true in the coming century. Economic decisions and policies will be framed with regard to an ever expanding information set. Insurance policies can be framed to pay out not just in response to easily verified sudden accidents, but also in terms of measures of changes in economic value or earnings potential, measures that are not vulnerable to moral hazard.

The advantages of better data collection for financial risk management have been developing for quite some time. It was 100 years ago, in 1913, that the United States launched its consumer price index for the express purpose of settling (labor) contracts. It was then possible to create financial contracts in real terms that would be meaningful to the broad population, and so then we began to see inflation-indexed contracts and financial instruments that offered a real gain in human welfare. It was in the Great Depression in the 1930s that the concept of gross national product (GNP) was first articulated, and we now have the early beginnings of risk management tools that make use of that, most recently, the issuance by the troubled Greek government of gross domestic product (GDP) warrants to raise money in a way that reduces their risks.[5] But GDP is hardly the end-all as a measure of economic welfare. In the next century, we ought to see a massive proliferation of indexes that indicate someone's welfare or lack thereof, and all of these indexes may be bases for risk management.

Big data create a risk that some risks, formerly insurable, may become uninsurable because the outcome may become known to insurers. For example, genetic testing might reveal predispositions to certain illnesses, and this knowledge could cause life insurance companies not to want to insure people with those risks or insure them at prohibitive premiums. But such an outcome can also be proscribed by law, as, for example, the U.S. Patient Protection Act of 2010 did for health insurance, and the big data and processing systems for it allow government regulators to verify that the law is being upheld.

Information Technology Will Shrink the Underground, Informal, and Shadow Economies

At this point in history, there are still substantial underground economic activities, even in the most advanced countries. People do not want their business dealings to be legitimized, since they wish to avoid taxation, regulation, or possible litigation. But in the next century, it will be increasingly difficult to hide cheating and evasion. As the total volume of information that is shared grows, people will be ever more easily caught in underground or shadow activities. Electronic money of one form or another is rapidly taking over, and the use of cash in a business transaction will begin to arouse suspicion.

We might include in underground activities the failure of home buyers around the world to report true real estate price transactions to authorities out of fear that their property taxes or other levies might be affected if they did. When there is not honest reporting, it is impossible to know what real estate prices are even doing in the aggregate. Once the prices are honestly reported, governments can formulate better policy regarding them, and private sector insurers can devise risk management contracts for real estate prices that are based on aggregates rather than own price, thereby diminishing moral hazard.

The key reason that the decline of the underground economy is important to risk management is that it allows the activities to enter big data, and once we can observe fluctuations in economic activity, we can devise mechanisms to control the risks it measures.

There Will Be Much Better Individual Identification and Still Privacy

If risk management is to be democratized, to deal with the risks that individuals really care about, risks that affect their livelihoods, then the individuals need to be tied to databases of information about them. Throughout traditional economies, the reputation and identity of individual people was discovered by letters of introduction, pocket identification cards, passports, and, more primitive, keeping people around who could recognize others' faces. But those methods did not allow people to be connected to databases of information about them. Modern computer biometrics can achieve such a linkage, and some time in this century, we might expect this to be available.

At the same time, computer technology must allow people to maintain their privacy. Digital technology of the future will allow people to divulge to others with whom they would have business dealings any level they desire of disclosure and to prevent those who receive the information from easily leaking the information to others.

Identification systems will be national (especially as to prevent terrorist activities) or privately issued. As identification systems become more secure (and more stable over the years), people will be better able to make enforceable long-term contracts involving their income and their property.

For example, they will be able to sell shares in their own future income, as Milton Friedman once proposed and then dismissed as unworkable because of enforcement problems.[6] Indentured servitude, a common institution in centuries past, was an economically useful kind of contract, but with too many humanitarian problems to survive into the present. But new and better forms of long-term commitment may again play a role in effective risk management of the next century

There Will Be an Ability to Make Much More Complex Financial Contracts

Information technology reduces the costs of monitoring and enforcing contracts, since much of this can now be handled mechanically by computers. As accounts are settled electronically, a contract can become at its inception a computer program to automatically make its terms a reality. This means that the contracts can be tailored more precisely to the needs of the contracting parties, and risk management can be more successful.

As the next century unfolds, we can hope to see that complex contracts can also refer to and interact appropriately with information about other such contracts. Consider some of the financial contracts we have today. For example, it is possible now for mortgage originators to search mortgage records to find out if a property has already been mortgaged to someone else. There are also credit reports available online that summarize a potential mortgagor's other loan contracts, as well as payment performance.

In the future, with big data suppliers supplying yet more information about individuals' activities, including rental agreements, employment contracts, and income risk management contracts, all of these pieces of information will be usable. A computer with capabilities close to artificial intelligence could keep track in an intelligent way, with all contracts, and thereby permit more effective contracting for fulfilling its role in risk management.

There Will Be No World Government, But There Will Be Stronger World Financial Institutions

A world government has been an idea stressed by many, but it continues to face immense obstacles. The League of Nations, established in 1919 and shut down in 1946, only the rudimentary of beginnings, was considered a failure. It was pushed aside by an attempt at developing a Neuordnung, starting in the 1930s under Adolf Hitler. The world war certainly left the whole concept of world government in shambles. The United Nations did emerge in 1945 from this conflict and has had some conspicuous successes.[7] But it has an annual budget in recent years of only about $5 billion, about the same as a single large-city police department. The G-20 countries have shown some remarkable new levels of international cooperation but still have no permanent secretariat or staff.

The real growth over the past century has been in the development of international financial institutions, with the Bank for International Settlements in 1930; the International Monetary Fund in 1944; the World Bank in 1944, which developed into the much larger World Bank Group; the InterAmerican Development Bank in 1959; the Asian Development Bank in 1966; the International Swaps and Derivatives Association in 1985; the World Trade Organization in 1995; and the International Accounting Standards Board in 2001. Even the United Nations has become involved in promoting good international financial institutions, through its Economic and Social Council, and in collaboration with partners in its Development Cooperation Forum, launched in 2007. If the trends continue, the international financial institutions will grow in size, and they will facilitate much more complex international financial contracts. This is significant, since so much of the important risk sharing that can add to human welfare is at the international level. The major risks of the next century that I describe here are likely to hit certain countries much more than others, and unless risk can be shared across countries, proper risk sharing cannot be achieved.

Financial arrangements can and historically often do outlive the governments under which they are made. That is because people inherently place some respect on financial arrangements that were made honestly and with good purpose, even after some of the bitterest wars. At the end of World War I, Germany was saddled with stiff reparations payments, but these were imposed in an orderly way, to be paid by orderly taxation of the German people, not by outright cancellation of financial contracts. When a radical Islamic government replaced the shah of Iran, it did not cancel government pension obligations incurred under the shah. When the white minority government in South Africa was replaced by a government that represented the black majority as well, it did not abrogate financial contracts. Of course, we can find other examples where a change in government did cause abrogation of financial contracts, notably with the revolutions that led to the Soviet Union and Communist China. The point is that financial contracts can often survive major changes in governments, and people can give substantial probability that their contracts will be upheld even after a major change in government.

Thus, too, in the next century, some critical financial risk sharing can be made across countries even if there is sometimes political chaos and the collapse of governments. This, combined with the other factors and information technology described in this section, implies some likely success in major new international risk sharing and in managing the most significant risks of the next century.

How the Important Risks Will Be Managed Better Using Financial and Information Technology

Information technology advances like those described in just described make way for any number of new risk management techniques.

Financial Devices to Deal with Long-Term Risks to Income Streams

Disability insurance today is a major weapon against economic inequality, but it is limited in its ability by the limitation of information on exogenous risks to economic status. In order to deal with a serious moral hazard problem, disability insurance has limited insured risks to those that can be traced to particular physical disabilities that cannot easily be feigned and that a doctor can document.

In the future, though, we must recognize that the ability of an individual to earn a livelihood is subject to numerous shocks, and the most important are shocks to that person's income. Indeed, one of those shocks might be, in the next century, the shock of being replaced by a computer. Fear of such eventualities can stymie individual initiative and make people fearful of specializing in their training and their careers, since they now bear all the career risk. In the next century, we can imagine that they will make career choices with the knowledge that they no longer have to bear all the risks.

It is reasonable to suppose, then, that as information technology becomes more thoroughly exploited, privately issued disability insurance will broaden into a much more comprehensive, privately issued livelihood insurance that insures an individual against losses to the market value of the individual's services.[8]

All of the factors described in the preceding section will in the future make it easier for insurance companies to depart from traditional limits on insurance so that individuals' livelihood risks can in fact be insured. The wider access to big data without invading privacy, along with the decline in the underground economy, means that they can develop measures of the success of individual careers and index numbers of occupational compensation that are much better and more granular than those available today and can serve as the basis for far more complex insurance contracts.

Risk management contracts taken on by individuals would likely follow them wherever they go (to whichever country) if international financial laws are enforced properly. Then they cannot evade obligations by emigrating.

Risk management contracts taken out by individuals could someday lead to a world where livelihood insurance policy premiums depend sensitively on the career choices that the insured has made. In a big data world, the prices implicit in the policies could become useful in making career choices, and people may be freed up to take on riskier career choices if the risk is uncorrelated so that the policies are not expensive. There would likely also develop futures markets for occupational incomes that help facilitate the provision of livelihood insurance. A whole new dimension of life fulfillment can be achieved by creating such markets.

Protections against Acts of War and Terrorism

Wars and terrorism appear to be among the biggest risks that we face in the next century because of the proliferation of weapons of mass destruction (WMD), notably nuclear, biological, chemical, and radiological (NBCR) weapons. U.S. Senator Richard Lugar surveyed over eighty national security experts, asking them to assess the risk.[9] The average expert assessment of the probability over the next ten years of a nuclear attack against a city or other target somewhere in the world was 29.2 percent, of a biological attack 32.6 percent, of a chemical attack 30.5 percent, and of a radiological attack, 39.8 percent. We are considering here the next 100 years, and for that, surely the probabilities are much larger.

The doomsday clock published in the *Bulletin of the Atomic Scientists* has been uncomfortably close to midnight since it was created in 1948 to assess the risks of the proliferation of nuclear weapons—risks not only of war but of terrorism or even accidental detonation. It has ranged from two minutes to midnight in 1953, when the United States tested its hydrogen bomb, to seventeen minutes to midnight in 1991, when the Soviet Union was dissolved. Their clock is now at five minutes to midnight.

Insurance companies traditionally exclude acts of war from covered risks, but there has been some progress in making such risks insurable. The problem has been that such risks tend to be correlated, creating big potential losses for insurance companies, and so they may be bankrupted by a bad outcome. This means that some government intervention is needed, and that purchase of insurance might best be compulsory so that people who see their property less at risk do not exit the scheme out of concern for higher premiums. Or the government might facilitate financial risk management vehicles, such as catastrophe bonds, that serve the same purpose.

Since no major WMD event has happened since the Hiroshima and Nagasaki bombings of 1945, there is public complacency. But history shows that such complacency disappears after some of the events are observed. For example, with the prodding of Winston Churchill after he personally experienced the German Blitz on London and saw the damage it was causing, affecting some properties catastrophically and leaving others completely spared, the U.K. Parliament passed the War Damage Act in 1941, with compulsory insurance for buildings. Though it came only late in the Blitz, it was retroactive. It was only a temporary plan, with high insurance premia reflecting the immediate war danger, not a plan for the longer future with more ill-defined war risks.

After the September 11, 2001, terrorist attacks on the United States, the U.S. Congress passed the Terrorist Risk Insurance Act (TRIA, 2002) to make it possible for people to get insurance against further such acts through government assumption of most of the risk. However, the act specifically excluded coverage of an attack that "is committed as part of the course of a war declared by the Congress." Moreover, the initial act expired after just three years (though it has since been renewed to 2014) and was capped at $100 billion, or about 1 percent of GDP when the law was passed. In a study of TRIA, Kunreuther et al. stressed deficiencies of the program, including a vulnerability to gaming the system by insurance companies.[10] Designing such insurance is a nontrivial matter, and we can expect to see better and more comprehensive designs in the future.

These past examples of war and terrorism risk insurance are confined to individual countries. But individual countries are too small to really manage these risks, which may be visited with great intensity on single countries. We can hope or expect to see international marketplaces for such risk to develop, placing higher costs of risk management on the more endangered countries. Israel and the United States, for example, face much more risk of nuclear attack than do many other countries. Still, so long as risk management contracts are put in place in advance for the long term, it is still largely unknown who will be most vulnerable, and so risk management can still work.

Assuming that the historic trend toward better insurance continues and given the likely stimulus for such insurance by actual WMD events, we can reasonably expect to see arrangements for much better coverage of such important risks, and we might suppose that if current trends toward the democratization of risk management continue, they will be made. Once we get the insurance industry involved in managing such risks, we will also see collateral benefits in terms of improved safety measures. In casualty insurance today, insurance inspectors and underwriters play a very useful role in assessing risks and providing a strong and present incentive for the insured to correct the risk now rather than defer and procrastinate.

Insurance is not completely hopeless even against NBCR weapons, the dreaded prospect of the next century. Insurance companies would be incentivized to think better how to minimize damage, for example, by enforcing better building codes, arranging for and paying for transport of people to dispersed safe areas, and then planning for cleanup and rebuilding after the event. Once insurance companies have an interest in preventing damage from such attacks, they may become a resource toward minimizing their impact.

Insurance against Environmental Risks Such as Global Warming

The risk of global warming, with all its attendant problems for the food supply and livability of certain climates, is only one of many long-term risks to the environment that should be managed in the future in part through suitable insurance and hedging devices. Other long-term risks that come to mind, some related to global warming, others not, include rising sea levels; increased risk of hurricanes and tropical storms; increased fungal damage to homes; damage to the ozone layer, which might cause dangerous levels of ultraviolet light; ocean acidification; as well as economic changes such as the adoption of biofuels that might push up food prices and threaten the poorest people. Other such risks that we can hardly imagine today will be discovered over the course of the next 100 years as more and more emerging countries attempt to reach the standard of living of advanced countries and put unprecedented strains on the environment

Standard insurance policies do not cover the risk of such increased risk. If hurricanes become more common in certain hurricane-prone areas, due, say, to global warming, homeowners in those areas will see their insurance premiums rise. There is no insurance today against rising premiums since the insurance policies are themselves short term.

Jaffee, Kunreuther, and Michel-Kerjan have argued that we need a new kind of homeowners' insurance, which they call long term-insurance (LTI), that protects homeowners against rising insurance premia because of long-term changes in environmental risks.[11] This will compensate those who turn out to be more harmed by unforeseen environmental catastrophes, shifting resources to the losers from the insurance premia of those less affected. Moreover, the insurance companies will put higher premia on insurance policies in geographical areas that can be predicted to be more harmed, thereby creating the correct incentives for people not to locate there.

Jaffee and his coauthors offer some theories as to why we have not seen such LTI in the past, suggesting that we will probably see it in the future. One problem has been that traditional regulators, who see themselves as advocates for short-run consumer interests, are reluctant to allow the higher premiums today that LTI would require. This narrow-mindedness of regulators should diminish as the environmental risks grow more tangible. Another reason is that in the absence of any long-term insurance today, there are no strong associated institutions of reinsurance or hedging of long-term risks, and so it is difficult for insurers to manage their risks. This problem could one day be solved by governments, which can, as with TRIA, mandate that insurance companies offer coverage.

Management of the Risk of Rising Inequality
The privately issued livelihood insurance described for individuals who choose specific occupations may not be adequate to protect society as a whole against major changes in the demand for the services that people of various situations can provide. There is a societal risk as well, one that the next generation will be born into a more unequal society. It is a risk that the

unlucky of the future can do nothing to insure against since it happened before they were born. Something akin to government social insurance against major longstanding risks to the income distribution of our society may be also adopted.

As I argued in *New Financial Order*, governments in the future may wish to index their income tax systems to inequality.[12] Progressive tax systems are already a substantial weapon against economic inequality. But there is no plan in place to make the tax system more progressive in the event of worsening inequality. Governments might legislate a system of response in future tax rates to future inequality. They could specify in the tax code that if, at any future date, inequality should pass some threshold of increased severity (as measured for example by the Lorenz curve), taxes would automatically increase on higher-income people and be lowered on lower-income people. This would make handling an emerging problem of increased inequality much easier politically. It is much easier to handle a problem of rising inequality before it happens than to wait until the new winners and losers are known and inequality is an established fact.

Such an inequality indexation scheme would be essentially a matter of risk management, a sort of insurance policy, as long as it is instituted before it is even known whether inequality gets really worse. Such a scheme may prevent some of our worst fears: economic changes that produce a highly unequal society. Whether or not inequality indexation is the right response, some planned response to rising inequality in the next century is surely needed, for the risk of substantial increases in inequality looms large.

The concern about technological unemployment due to computers' replacing jobs was expressed at the very dawn of the computer age. MIT mathematician and computer pioneer Norbert Wiener expressed this concern in his 1948 book, *Cybernetics*:

Long before Nagasaki and the public awareness of the atomic bomb, it had occurred to me that we were here in the presence of another social potentiality of unheard-of importance for good and for evil. There is no rate of pay at which a United States pick-and-shovel laborer can live that is low enough to compete with the work of a steam shovel as an excavator. The modern industrial revolution is similarly bound to devalue the human brain, at least in its simpler and more routine decisions. Of course, just as the skilled carpenter, the skilled mechanic, and the skilled dressmaker have in some degree survived the first industrial revolution, so the skilled scientist and the skilled administrator may survive the second. However, taking the second revolution as accomplished, the average human being of mediocre attainments or less has nothing to sell that is worth anyone's money to buy.[13]

Wassily Leontief, who is remembered for his studies of the input–output structure of the economy, echoed a similar concern thirty-five years later:

Computers and robots replace humans in the exercise of mental functions in the same way as mechanical power replaced them in the performance of physical tasks. As time goes on, more and more complex mental functions will be replaced by machines. . . . This means that the role of humans as the most important factor of production is bound to diminish in the same way that the role of horses in agricultural production was first diminished and then eliminated by the introduction of tractors.[14]

The fact that the disaster Wiener and Leontieff worried about has not come yet is little consolation: computer technology has been growing so much faster than other economic forces that we know of that it may be about to become vastly important.

Computer technology seems to be replacing an unheard of number of basic jobs. It was long ago that most telephone operators were replaced by electronic dialing systems. So too were reference librarians who help patrons use the library to answer questions replaced by Internet search engines. Even today we have global positioning systems and adaptive cruise control that seem poised to make possible driverless cars, thereby potentially eliminating all jobs as drivers. How much further will this go over the course of the next century?

Other kinds of jobs will certainly crop up that are created by computer technology, though it strains our imagination to try to spell out what they will be. It seems we may be facing a change that Jeremy Rifkin has described as "so vast in scale that we are barely able to fathom its ultimate impact."[15]

But this result is not necessarily terrible as long as we make some provision so that standards of living are not horrendous for lower-income people. If all goes well, computers will not have replaced people in the next century, as many fear today. Instead, information technology will allow people to interact better and achieve their goals better. Essential to this is that we will have markets for many more factors that are not even recognized today.

Advanced Risk Management, Finance, and Insurance Will Make for Better Achievement of Personal Goals

Labor income available for consumption and labor itself are the two key entries into the utility function concept that has underpinned most economic theory. The next century seems to pose extraordinary risks for these: jobs may be threatened and inequality may worsen, even in the long term. But in preparing to deal with such risks, we need to step back from this simple labor-leisure paradigm and consider the risks in a broader, more psychologically informed framework.

The economists' simple distinction between labor and leisure, with the presumption that labor is displeasing and leisure is pleasing, is easily found wanting. That this is so can be seen by examining the words roughly meaning "work" in our language. In English the verb *to work* exists somewhere near the middle of a continuum of similar words that range from disagreeable to agreeable: *to slave, to labor, to execute, to perform, to dabble, to putter, to achieve.*

There is such a temptation to yield to the impulse to work *for* personal goals that work can be an addiction, as in the word *workaholic.* Not only do many people voluntarily work extra hours on their jobs, but they also develop frivolous activities that resemble work, as with the high-income businessperson who wants to mow the lawn or fix the door on a weekend, even though others could do the work more effectively and cheaply.

We may see in the future, as people grow familiar with a world that requires much less traditional work, a focus that changes from the availability of opportunities for work to opportunities to try to reach personal goals. The goals will never be specified by our computers, so computers, in conjunction with societal institutions, will be aids to such work.

Fortunately, the uncertainty about one's ability to achieve personal goals itself is something that information technology in the next century can deal with. The risks that obsess us today may largely vanish. We might expect to find that in the next century, we will have a better sense of meaning and fulfillment in our lives

The Time Frame for Change

This chapter, and this book itself, has a time horizon of 100 years, far longer than is commonplace in planning for the future. Thinking about such a long horizon encourages thought about fundamental changes—not just immediate legislative proposals or business ideas that would be practicable today.

Many of the changes in risk management that I have discussed here are likely to unfold over a really long time frame. History suggests this. The principle of insurance was already employed in some insurance products in ancient times, and so it is two thousand years old. Insurance began to blossom in the 1600s, with the birth of probability theory and actuarial science, but it did not take hold for large sections of the population until the twentieth century. The principle of hedging and portfolio diversification, understood at some level centuries ago, did not develop into a science until the second half of the twentieth century, and yet it still shows serious inadequacies, as revealed by the recent financial crisis.

Advancing risk management along these lines over such a long time can be thought of as a continuation of a historic trend toward the democratization and humanization of our society. The risks that I have discussed here are probably not going away; they are inherent in the kind of economic progress that people the world over demand, and we cannot prevent all catastrophes. But we can, and likely will, make use of our information technology, ability to identify and track people and their risks, and make and enforce much more complicated and long-term contracts, to reduce the impact of such catastrophes on human welfare.

9 Stray Thoughts on How It Might Go

Robert M. Solow

The Last Hundred Years Are Hard Enough

One hundred years is a very long time, perhaps not on the evolutionary timescale, but certainly on the economic. The conventional estimate of real national income per person in the United States in 1910 puts it at 19.2 percent of its value in 2010. That represents an average annual growth rate of 1.66 percent. There were no national accounts in 1910, so the number itself is doubtful. Besides, it is not clear how to translate that numerical abstraction into a comparison of lived experience or "standard of living."

We have a feeling for the 2010 figure of $43,000 per person. We know roughly what it makes possible and what it excludes. The 1910 average of $8,300 per person ("in constant prices") is much foggier in content, as well as less accurate. Much of the contents of a 2010 standard of living was not available in 1910, was not even thinkable. For that matter, even a 1910 apple was rather a different piece of fruit from the 2010 model going under the same name. How could someone in 1910 have had any grasp of what economic life would be like a century later, even with a good guess at the growth rate of real GDP? The answer to that question was not knowable. I do not mean just the answer was hidden from view, but that it had not been determined. Nevertheless, if Rip van Winkle Jr. had fallen sleep in 1910 and awakened in 2010, he would have been surprised and bewildered, but it would be recognizable human life that he was seeing. The experience of Rip van Winkle III will presumably be similar.

The Next Hundred Are Harder

Those are qualitative difficulties; there are intrinsic quantitative problems as well. Something that starts equal to 1 and grows at an average rate of

1.2 percent a year for 100 years will be equal to 3.30 at the end of the century. If instead it had grown at 1.6 percent a year, it would have ended at 4.89, larger by half. Think of this something as productivity, or total factor productivity, or even income per person. The interval from 1.2 to 1.6 is a plausible range of growth rates. In fact, I could have easily chosen a wider interval with a more dramatic difference in end points. But no one today can seriously argue for one number rather than another in that interval as a forecast for productivity growth over the next 100 years. There may be no harm in guessing, but a mere guess is not an argument. The only justification for making such a forecast today is that you will not live to know how wrong you were. That may not be justification enough.

Nevertheless, I will carry on a bit longer, though I will soon raise further questions. Median family income in the United States is currently a little more than $60,000. Is it possible to imagine that the corresponding figure for 2113 should be four times that, in constant prices? (That is a bit less than a fivefold increase in GDP per person from 1910 to 2010. At this point, averages or even medians seem inadequate, and one wants to know more about distribution, but never mind.) Yes, I suppose it is imaginable. In current American political discourse, perhaps not the acme of sobriety, an annual income of $250,000 is described as the top of the "middle class." No one seems to laugh. Why would the median family a century from now not be able to achieve and enjoy what passes today for a high middle-class standard of living?

In thinking about all this, one should keep in mind the steady shift of consumer spending toward services and away from material goods. In 1960, 47 percent of all (nominal) consumer expenditure went to services; by 2009 that share had risen to 68 percent. The contrast with 1910 would be even sharper. That shift is likely to continue; one expects education, personal care, tourism, recreation, financial services, and the like to have a high-income elasticity of demand, though health care is complicated and remains to be settled. Even so, the pace of shift to services is uncertain over so long a period, with so large a potential increase in income, and so much possibility for changes in preferences and technology.

Hours of Work

A major uncertainty, with important implications for the pattern of consumption, has to do with the evolution of decisions about work and leisure.

During the first half of the twentieth century, the average annual hours of a full-time American worker tended to fall slowly but fairly surely. Then forty or fifty years ago, that tendency seemed to diminish substantially or disappear. Nowadays American (and Japanese and Korean) workers put in many more hours per year than counterparts in the high-income countries of Europe. Average annual hours worked in the United States are about a quarter higher than in France and Germany. There is controversy about the causes of this discrepancy.

One view often expressed is that the source of the difference is "cultural." Americans like to get ahead. In a consumerist society, that means making more money and spending more. Europeans may be less interested in stuff and more interested in leisure. (It is sometimes forgotten that some popular uses of leisure require quite a lot of stuff.) When increasing productivity compels a choice, Americans are generally inclined to choose more goods, Europeans more likely to choose a shorter workday and longer vacations. The other view is that the all-in tax rate on the income from a marginal hour worked is considerably higher in Europe than in the United States. Even without any major differences in preferences or social norms, routine behavior responses would lead Europeans to work fewer hours than Americans.

There is probably truth in both arguments. Personally I find it easy to believe that the transition to much higher incomes will lead to a shorter work year in the United States, especially if the age of retirement increases. That would at least replicate the difference between 1910 and today. But there is no solid basis for a guess.

But then what about the work year of a unit of real capital, a "machine"? There is no automatic answer. Suppose, just to simplify, that the size of the labor force remains constant. Then a reduction in average hours worked per year is an equal proportional reduction in total hours worked. Suppose we think in terms of given capital intensity (total machine hours/total labor hours). So total machine hours falls too. By definition, the stock of machines is given by total machine hours/average hours worked per machine. One extreme is that average hours worked per machine remains constant (if all machines worked continuously, 24/7). Then the necessary stock of capital falls too. At the other extreme, one can imagine that the work year of a machine falls with the work year of labor (e.g., if "my" machine works only when I am working). Then the necessary stock of capital is unchanged. Anything in between is clearly possible.

I think this is the natural range of possibilities, although there is no logical or physical reason that the work year of a machine should not actually increase, say. But it would seem more likely that increased leisure over the next century should be accompanied by a smaller stock of capital (per worker), smaller gross investment (per worker), and thus a larger share of consumption in GDP. Of course, this tendency will almost certainly be off-set by an ongoing increase in capital intensity, even in the service sector. Obviously there are other, totally moot, considerations. Will leisure time activities be especially capital intensive (grandiose hotels, enormous cruise ships) or the opposite (growing marigolds, reading poetry)? Show me an economist with a strong opinion about these things, and I will show you that oxymoron: a daredevil economist.

Climate, Environment, Resources

There is still a potentially larger uncertainty to be reckoned with even if we continue to think only of the already developed world. One hundred years is long enough for the effects of global warming to limit economic growth—perhaps marginally, but perhaps drastically. The model predictions are themselves uncertain; on top of that, it is impossible to know how policy will respond or how those responses will affect measured output and income. As of now, one would have to say: hardly at all. But the policy response might have to change in the course of a century as climate events unfold.

Apart from climate change, other induced environmental effects on air, water, land use, and urban livability may manifest themselves and lead to changes in economic life. The continued and expanded use of nonrenew-able natural resources could lead to either effective exhaustion or sharply rising relative prices, either of which would alter growth prospects over a century. Simple extrapolation will hardly do if the goal is to look far ahead. One interesting reason is the shift to services. Casual (excessively casual?) thought suggests that most services substitute human capital for material capital and resource products. (I inserted the word *most* because I have an appointment with my excellent and all kinds of capital-intensive dentist tomorrow!) If the world were to go Voltairean and choose mainly to cultivate gardens, the input-output table could change a lot. Production would put less strain on the scarce resources base and the waste disposal capacity of the environment.

Inequality

The current episode (if it is only an episode) of increasing income inequality in the United States dates from the 1970s. The odds that it will continue must depend on its deeper economic or social sources. Is it primarily a by-product of the growth of the financial sector and its proclivity to pay enormous sums to successes and failures alike? Or does it have something to do with an underlying market trend in the relative compensation of labor, human capital, tangible capital, and entrepreneurship? And I have not mentioned other possible influences, like international trade, migration, the decay of labor unionism, or the distribution of educational opportunity. Those are hard questions, and any estimate of the future and the appropriate policy response (which may alter the future) depends on the answer.

I will focus on the second possibility, shifts in the remuneration of labor and capital, not because I am convinced that it is the right one, but because it is what economists are used to thinking about. It is clear that something substantial has been happening. We used to think the proportion in which income is divided between labor and capital as one of the great constants on the economy. Not since 1960, however: there has been a definite tilt against labor income. We can see that from two different vantage points.

First, since 1960 the real compensation of labor in the nonfarm business sector has lagged well behind productivity. Output per hour rose by a factor of 2.82; real compensation per hour (which includes benefits) rose only by a factor of 1.94. Second, a quite different set of figures tells us that compensation of labor was 72.1 percent of all nominal personal income in 1960; in 2009, it was 63.7 percent. On either scale, this may seem like a minor change. By the standards of the past, however, it is high drama. If the 1960 proportion had ruled in 2010, roughly $1 trillion of income would have gone to labor that in fact went to other forms of income. (I am not bothering to disentangle business cycle effects from trend effects. Any way you slice it, this is a big deal.)

Neither set of numbers tells us exactly what we want to know. But it is unmistakable that nonlabor income, whether return on tangible capital investment, rewards of entrepreneurship, monopoly profit, or something else, has gained at the expense of labor income (which presumably includes much of the return on human capital). One way or another, this is the outcome of complicated market forces.

Can This Go On?

Should we expect this drift to continue into the future? For that we would need to know more about those "market forces." Some of the eligible market forces include (1) changes in the ease with which capital can be substituted for labor as economy-wide capital intensity increases, (2) changes in the nature of new technology, (3) changes in the industrial composition of aggregate output, (4) changes in the amount and distribution of monopoly power, not to mention institutional changes like (5) decay of unionism and (6) the balance of political power. "All of the above" is the easy, if unenlightening, answer.

In the context of speculations about the next 100 years, it is interesting to think about the implications if this trend were to continue. If the underlying source is embedded in the composition of aggregate output and the nature of technology, then the shift away from labor income would be hard to reverse. We are not good at large-scale redistribution of income, and we do not seem to be getting any better. So one possibility is a remorseless reduction in the share of income going to human labor, probably accompanied by increasing inequality. (Absolute wages could, of course, continue to rise.) This story is reminiscent of the recurrent bad dream of an economy in which robots do all the production, including the production of robots, with the proles on the outside looking in.

That is pushing the trend pretty far on no evidence. But even a moderate extrapolation would seem to call for a response. That might take the form of a democratization of capital: as wage income shrinks (relative to the total), ordinary people could draw more of their income from capital. The capital would have to come in part from their own saving—for example, funded pensions—and in part from capital accumulated on their behalf by the state, maybe in the form of mutual funds. You realize that this is a fantasy. The reality will be more pedestrian.

The Rest of the World

Everything I have said so far has been about the rich, developed countries. But of course most of the world's population lives elsewhere, in the poor countries or in the emerging economies. For them, the puzzles take a different form: Will those economies stagnate or, if not, must they, will they, industrialize before deindustrializing, more or less following the historical pattern? Or alternatively, with the example of the rich countries in front of them, available for imitation, will they go from potato farmer to couch potato in a much smaller number of generations? Obviously there is no law of economics about ontogeny recapitulating phylogeny. Nevertheless, it seems clear that some emerging economies will, for at least some time, have a manifest comparative advantage in labor-intensive manufacturing.

There are several related reasons for expecting development to take this form. If development succeeds at all, if more economies "emerge," the world demand for manufactures and other material goods will certainly grow rapidly. All those people with rising incomes will have to accumulate household goods: houses and their contents, cars or other means of personal transportation, the various public and private goods that accompany at least slightly affluent urbanization, and so on. Satisfying that demand will require investment in productive capacity, much of it presumably local.

When (or if) this happens, it will happen at a twenty-first-century level of technology. Even so, because many of the goods in question are not terribly complex and because a large supply of low-wage semiskilled labor is available, the likeliest outcome is the growth of local manufacturing, construction, and similar sectors in the next cohort of emerging economies, just as happened with its predecessors. These industries will be more sophisticated than those that characterized earlier industrialization. They should provide a natural training ground for the literacy-related and numeracy-related skills that will later, sooner than in the past, lay the basis for the normal shift to services.

Of course, we are all aware of the appearance of tradable-service sectors in countries like India and China. They seem to be fairly small in employment terms, however, and not (or not yet) the signal of a massive shift in comparative advantage. One would not be surprised, however, to see this shift occur faster than it did with the current advanced economies. I suspect that much depends on the speed and efficiency with which the currently poor countries can organize their educational systems and, what is just as important and maybe more difficult, arrange for meritocratic social mobility. I would not know how to quote the odds. This is not to deny that there could be other success stories, like the Bangalore-based IT sector in India, but it is a good guess that this will not be the norm.

The trajectory of the world economy will depend on the speed with which those countries grow and the qualitative nature of their growth. I am referring to such obvious matters as the drain they place on the world's supply of water and other natural resources, on the care they take with environmental amenities (including their contribution to climate change), and, above all, on their success in speeding up the demographic transition to slower-growing or stationary populations.

How Will It Add Up?

One has to suppose that the successful developers in the world economy will be able to grow faster than the old industrial countries were able to do in the nineteenth and twentieth centuries. The possibility of technological catch-up and the relatively easy availability of a flow of investment capital from the already rich world are a major advantage accelerating the growth of the latecomers. The major uncertainties appear to be political. I could go on at length about governance issues because I know so little about them. It is enough to observe that the passage from national poverty to sustained economic growth requires favorable policy commitments over long periods. Anarchy, violence, cronyism, and corruption are not features of a successful trajectory.

Eventual resource scarcity and environmental stress (especially climate change) are another matter. No one can know with any precision how many people can be supported in the world at a standard of living anything like that of the currently advanced countries. As always, that depends on an implicit race between scarcity and new technology. Demography and technology are forces that are at least partially open to influence by public policy.

I guess this sounds modestly optimistic. Keynes was famously optimistic and worried less about things like excess population and environmental stress in the developing world. He dwelled more on the likelihood that as incomes increased and work time fell, ordinary people would be at a loss to find things to do with their leisure. I do not fully subscribe to Jeremy Bentham's opinion that pushpin (whatever that may be) is as good as poetry. But that particular worry is fairly low on my list.

10   The Geoengineered Planet

Martin L. Weitzman

If there is one genuinely natural bridge spanning the chasm between now and a century from now, I think it is climate change. We who are here now can envision only the foundation of this bridge, and we see this foundation but through a glass darkly. Even so, we can make out enough features to sense that something big and possibly ominous might be in the making on the distant horizon.

In this chapter, I speculate on the subject of the future of climate change. In particular, I focus on the nexus between humanity and nature as viewed through the lens of geoengineering. Unless there is some currently unforeseeable revolutionary technological breakthrough making large-scale noncarbon energy generation much less expensive in the future, it is extremely difficult for me to imagine a binding international agreement being reached on significant reductions in carbon emissions. By contrast, the temptation may become very great for some medium-developed nation feeling itself under climate change siege to unilaterally geoengineer itself (and the planet) out of high temperatures by seeding the stratosphere with sunshine-reflecting particles because it is so extraordinarily cheap. Such a combination gives rise to two simultaneous public goods problems, creating what I will call the twin externality dilemma of climate change. This twin externality dilemma, and what it might entail, is the central subject of my futuristic chapter.

Frankly, this futuristic intellectual foray belongs in the realm of science fiction. It is much more speculation than prediction. While based on contemporary ideas, it is not a deterministic consequence of them. My hope is that it is good, or at least decent, science fiction, meaning, for me, that it induces us to think big on the connection between the present and the future while also thinking big on the human and natural conditions we find ourselves embedded in. I also hope the narrative is at least slightly entertaining as well. So this is going to be a big-think piece, opinionated, speculative, a bit rambling, and largely without endnotes.

By narrowing my focus (here to a story about geoengineering and climate change), I believe I am following the broad spirit of Keynes's own short essay, "Economic Possibilities for Our Grandchildren." In my view, Keynes did not stray especially widely in his thoughts, considering the vast potential scope of the subject. Instead, he focused primarily on the particular theme of what it might mean to work less and enjoy leisure more, which for him was a key issue about the distant future. His relative narrowness was probably a wise strategic decision, given the potential immensity of distant future possibilities and the temptation to wander all over the map in exploring them. Here I try a similar narrowing tactic. I do not claim that climate change is the only important issue that the world will face a century from now. Given the vast miasma of uncertainty surrounding the distant future, and especially surrounding climate change in the distant future, I cannot even be sure that this issue will turn out to be as important as I think it is likely to become. Suffice it to say that I have worked on the economics of climate change, that I think it is likely (if not surely) to be highly important for the future of the planet, and that I have a few rambling thoughts about what it all might mean.

Some scientists and others have argued that the geological epoch in which we now live is deserving of a new name, the *Anthropocene*. The basic idea is that we have arrived at a point in geological history where human beings are a prime mover, or even the dominant driver, of changes in the earth system's natural history, on a scale of what we often attribute to titanic underlying natural forces such as ice ages. Parts of this human-induced movement have been going on for some time. The human biomass of some 7 billion people exceeds the biomass of all other large species of animals combined, and indeed it is larger than many entire phyla of the animal kingdom. Our capture of energy for primary production is on the scale of a very large ecosystem. Our footprint on our human-altered planet's landscape is already huge. In all of natural history, no other single species has come anywhere near to dominating planet Earth as *Homo sapiens* has.

Yet it is the possibility—indeed the near inevitability—of human-induced climate change on an enormous planetary scale that, more than anything else, has motivated the concept of the Anthropocene epoch. I know from personal experience that it can take people a long time to accept the shocking notion that cumulative human emissions of greenhouse gases could be so powerful that they might profoundly change our climate. It can seem too counterintuitive that humans could be instigating global changes of such a magnitude. I think that this is a big part of the problem of accepting the reality of anthropogenic climate change.

The bare facts of climate change will be familiar to most readers. I review some salient features that seem to me particularly relevant for the purposes of where I want to go with this chapter.

Greenhouse gases warm the planet by trapping heat. The most important greenhouse gas by far is carbon dioxide. By massively burning carbon-based fossil fuels, which have been naturally deposited over the course of hundreds of millions of years, humans are emitting carbon dioxide at a rate that is unprecedented even on geological timescales. We know carbon dioxide levels almost exactly for the last 800,000 years from measuring tiny air bubbles trapped in layers of Antarctic ice cores. We are currently (in 2013) experiencing atmospheric carbon dioxide levels that are some 40 percent higher than the highest levels recorded in the previous 800,000 years. If we continue at roughly this growth rate for another century or so, we will likely attain levels of carbon dioxide between two and three times higher than the highest levels attained over the past tens of millions of years. From strong built-in inertias, temperatures and climate changes lag atmospheric carbon dioxide accumulations by centuries (or even millennia) and linger on for centuries (and even millennia) thereafter, even if emissions were to cease altogether. Where we will actually end up a century or so from now and what will be the subsequent consequences depends on many factors that are highly uncertain, but many of the prospects seem unnerving, especially if, as I fear, nothing much significant is done about carbon dioxide emissions.

In this timing sequence, there is a profound dilemma. By geological standards, these greenhouse gas changes are of unprecedented speed. Being geologically instantaneous, and therefore without precedent, what will happen next is highly uncertain and might well involve low-probability, high-impact catastrophic outcomes. However, by standards of a human lifetime, these centuries-spanning changes are incredibly slow, and therefore the consequences seem extremely remote to us. Humans have no experience and limited patience for dealing with even possibly catastrophic events that unfold this slowly. How much more sense it makes to deal now with the actual problems of today rather than the hypothetical problems of the distant future. So right from the beginning, a fight against global warming faces an unprecedented uphill battle against human nature to convince people to take seriously uncertain, seemingly hypothetical, events that will unfold over the course of centuries from now.

I think it is fair to say that as of today, the overall impact of climate change on the human condition, here and now, has thus far been very small. Climate change just has not yet had an impact on the average person's life. People are therefore being asked to sacrifice in the present in the name of something that to them is hypothetical, that they cannot detect now, whose exact impact is uncertain, and that will become an actual threat to everyday living only in the remote future, if at all. We just do not have experience in this sort of thing. Maybe civilizations that come after ours will have such experience with distant-future threats, but right now we do not.

I touched on the subject of possibly ruinous climate change. The essence of this particularly nasty problem is that there is no natural bound on how bad things might get as greenhouse gases pile up. It is difficult to draw a line in the sand and say that things can only get this bad and no worse. Climate change is unusual in potentially affecting the entire worldwide portfolio of utility by threatening to drive all of planetary welfare to disastrously low levels in the most extreme scenarios. With climate change, all of our eggs are in one basket and there is no obvious way to diversify this macrorisk. It really is possible to wreck the earth with a high enough concentration of greenhouse gases because of the potentially open-ended catastrophic reach of severe climate change. But what is a "high enough concentration of greenhouse gases" that might trigger ruinous climate change? We do not know. Everything is uncertain. We cannot control climate outcomes by controlling greenhouse gas concentrations. At best we can control only the probabilities of climate outcomes by controlling greenhouse gas concentrations. I do not think the world grasps the enormous magnitude of the uncertainties involved in predicting climate change under high-greenhouse-gas scenarios, a perennial source of irritation for a public suspicious of anything but crisp deterministic answers to "what if?" questions.

The massive structural uncertainties at the heart of climate change can seem overwhelming when they are aggregated together. The core problem is that if we keep emitting GHGs at current rates for another century or so, we will likely be so far outside the range of ordinary geological and human experience that we are unsure what processes will ultimately be unleashed and what will happen next.

The science and economics of climate change consist of a very long chain of tenuous inferences fraught with big uncertainties in every link. Begin with unknown greenhouse gas emissions. We do not know what we should take as a base-case trajectory for future greenhouse gas emissions. We do not know what the world is going to agree on as policy for limiting emissions. And even if the world agreed on some policy or another, there would remain big uncertainties about how available policy levers, like taxes, tradable permits, and standards, will affect actual greenhouse gas emissions.

Then there are big scientific uncertainties about how greenhouse gas flow emissions accumulate through the carbon cycle into atmospheric greenhouse gas stock concentrations. And even if we accurately knew the trajectory of future stocks of atmospheric greenhouse gases, a lot of uncertainty exists about how and when greenhouse gas stock concentrations translate into global average temperature changes. There are also great uncertainties about how global average temperature changes decompose into specific changes in regional and temporal weather patterns, which are much more unsure than any globally averaged number can capture. Here is about where the economic unknowns start to kick in. How are uncertainties about adaptations to, and mitigations of, climate change damages at a regional level translated into regional utility or welfare changes through an appropriate regional "damages function"? What values should be put on the alteration or destruction of existing ecosystems? How should regional utility changes be aggregated into a single worldwide utility function, and what should its overall properties be? What discount rate should be used to convert everything into expected present discounted values?

The result of this lengthy cascading of big uncertainties is a reduced form of truly stupendous uncertainty about the aggregate welfare impacts of climate change. And what I have enumerated here is only a partial list of all of the uncertainties. With climate change a century or so from now representing an extrapolation so far beyond the realms of past experience, there is a large potential scope for things going very wrong that we cannot now even envision—the notorious unknown unknowns whose role here is very plausibly nonnegligible. Such black swan events represent outliers that are difficult or even impossible to predict. And because there is no natural bound on how bad things might get with catastrophic climate change, some black swan events might have terrible consequences.

The issue of how to deal with the deep structural uncertainties in climate change would be completely different and immensely simpler if systemic inertias, like the time required for the system to naturally remove extra atmospheric carbon dioxide, were short, as is the case for many airborne pollutants like sulfur dioxide, nitrous oxides, and particulates. Then an important component of an optimal strategy might be along the lines of wait and see. With strong reversibility, an optimal climate change policy would logically involve (among other elements) waiting to learn how far out on the bad probability tail the planet will end up, followed by mid-course corrections if we seem to be headed for a disaster. Alas, the problem of climate change seems bedeviled at almost every turn by significant stock accumulation inertias—in atmospheric carbon dioxide, in the absorption of heat or atmospheric carbon dioxide by the oceans, and in many other relevant physical and biological processes, which are slow to respond to attempts at reversal. So the climate change problem is characterized by irreversibilities and the unsureness of being able to learn by our potential mistakes in enough time to reverse change-underlying conditions significantly.

The final background issue on climate change that I present concerns the massive public goods problem posed by this mother of all externalities. Although it is a global public good of immense overall magnitude, climate change has different and extremely uneven impacts on different regions of the world. As a generalization, the poorer and less developed countries are likely to suffer adverse impacts most acutely. Furthermore, when all is said and done, I personally think it will be expensive—perhaps very expensive—to replace a carbon-based energy technology with a non-carbon-based energy technology on a truly worldwide scale. Getting international agreement (with meaningful verification oversight and compliance penalties) on an effective unified strategy for combating global climate change seems like an overwhelmingly difficult task.

The upshot of this discussion of selected background issues on climate change is that I am pessimistic about the prospects for meaningful timely action on averting bad outcomes. Until people actually see and feel that climate change is adversely affecting their daily lives, I fear that not very much will be done about it. To what extent people will feel that climate change is adversely affecting their daily lives, at what future time they might feel this, what then might be done about it, and whether it might then be too late (or not) are all questions whose answers are plagued by such uncertainty that they are highly speculative. The one thing that I feel fairly secure in predicting is that hypothetical future threats of climate change will not be enough to create a serious worldwide coordinated attack on the problem until the frightening actual impact (or perhaps actual real imminent threat) of some scary geoevent mobilizes a genuine popular groundswell of bottom-up demand for action.

With this pessimistic backdrop, I next explore some of the issues raised by a geoengineered planet a century or so hence.

In one sense the term *geoengineering* might just reflect aspects of the Anthropocene epoch in which humans have already become a prime mover in the earth's natural history. This aspect of geoengineering is largely inadvertent, the accidental by-product of large-scale human planetary alterations for other aims. The other sense of geoengineering connotes purposeful action. This form of purposeful geoengineering is typically aimed at undoing the deleterious planetary alterations that we have already inadvertently geoengineered. More on this later.

To a large extent, we have already inadvertently geoengineered the planet. After all, the geologically instantaneous increase in concentrations of atmospheric GHGs constitutes a massive by-product of the burning of huge past deposits of fossil fuels being converted from carbon into carbon dioxide. So global warming itself is a kind of geoengineering. And if some of the proposed "solutions" to climate change problems were to make a dent in the burning of fossil fuels, they would of necessity involve converting large areas of the planet into wind farms, solar panel assemblages, carbon capture and storage facilities, and the like, with corresponding environmental impacts of their own.

Even without considering climate change, the agricultural need to feed a world population of some 7 billion people has necessitated a geoengineered landscape on a stupendous global scale. Furthermore, housing and transporting and providing work stations for 7 billion of the world's population has also required geoengineered agglomerations of massive proportions. These vast global-scale engineering works will be significantly expanded even more as China, India, and other developing countries seek ever higher standards of living and as the population of the world increases yet more in the coming century or so.

The upshot is that geoengineering with a big human footprint has been with us for some time and is likely to increase ferociously in the future, no matter how the climate changes. For sure, climate change introduces a whole new dimension to the idea of geoengineering, especially the idea of purposefully geoengineering the planet to undo the inadvertent geoengineering we are doing with massive greenhouse gas releases. There will be much more on this subject later. But the basic concept of massive human planetary alteration is already in place.

Thus, especially with, but even without, geoengineered climate change, humans and nature are already so intertwined that they are no longer separate entities. This is hardly an original thought on my part, but I think that the issue is likely to come to a head in the next century or so with the probable onset of serious climate change. The primary issue here will not so much concern humans preserving nature, but will be more about humans coevolving wisely with nature. I will have more to speculate on this subject when discussing geoengineering in the context of climate change. But this coevolution issue is sufficiently subtle and has snuck up on us so quietly that I want to make sure the idea is anchored by a specific example that is untainted by climate change.

I could have chosen any number of such examples of past large-scale coevolution of humans with nature, but the one I select here for concrete illustration is the North American tallgrass prairie. This vast ecosystem was almost completely destroyed within a generation when it was discovered how to get at the incredibly rich agricultural soils beneath the Midwest prairies with a steel moldboard plow. The North American tallgrass prairie was then nearly instantaneously plowed under for farmland, from end to end. I go into this example in some detail because I want to use it as a kind of paradigm.

What is today the most productive large farmland area in the world was a mere century and a half ago the largest virgin tallgrass prairie in the world. However, it turns out that the now-vanished tallgrass prairie ecosystem of the North American Midwest was itself a relatively recent phenomenon—less than ten thousand or so years old. If a farmer were forced to abandon rich Iowa farmland today, it would pass through several successional stages, with its climax vegetation reverting not to prairie but to some form of mature woodland. Prairie, rather than woodland, existed in the North American Midwest in the first place because of recurrent periodic fires. These well-documented large-scale burns were set by Native Americans. They were mostly deliberate and primarily for hunting purposes. Today what is called "prescribed burning" is a critical ingredient of all serious prairie restoration projects.

But what exactly is the prescribed burning trying to restore? It is not attempting to resurrect "nature" in the pure sense of what would have been there without human intervention in the first place. That would be a woodland climax ecosystem. Prairie restoration is trying to bring back an ecosystem that coevolved with human intervention. Is this tallgrass prairie ecosystem "natural" or "artificial"? Does restoring it represent reverence for wilderness or reverence for the past? Does it make a difference?

I think that the paradigm of the tallgrass prairie restoration dilemma may become ratcheted up to a central theme a century or so from now if and when large-scale climate change impacts are being felt. In such a tallgrass prairie paradigm writ large, the issue with climate change will not so much concern humans preserving nature as about humans coevolving wisely with nature. To portray sharply the conceivable magnitude of this distant-future dilemma in the climate change context, I purposely pick an extreme "what if?" example of a low-probability high-impact catastrophic possibility—and what might be the reaction to it a century or so from now.

Human-induced climate change is unusual because there is potentially unlimited downside liability. There is no market in which to short the planet as a hedge against catastrophic damages. To put some bite into this possibility, here is just one example of what might possibly go very wrong in a worst-case scenario.

This example of a potential catastrophe concerns possibly disastrous releases over the long run of bad-feedback components of the carbon cycle that are currently omitted from most general circulation models. The chief concern here is that there may be significant, if highly uncertain, supplementary components that conceptually should be added to the global warming feedbacks that are normally considered on shorter timescales. One omitted component is the possibly powerful self-amplification potential of greenhouse warming that is due to heat-induced releases of sequestered carbon. A vivid example is the huge volume of greenhouse gases currently trapped in tundra permafrost and other boggy soils, mostly as methane, a particularly potent greenhouse gas. A more remote, but even more danger-ously vivid, possibility, which in principle should also be included, is heat-induced releases of the even vaster offshore deposits of methane trapped in the form of clathrates.[1]

There is a very small but unknown positive probability over the long run (centuries to millennia) of having destabilized methane from these offshore clathrate deposits seep into the atmosphere if the temperature of the waters bathing the continental shelves increases just slightly. The amount of meth-ane involved is huge, although it is not precisely known. Most estimates place the carbon-equivalent content of methane hydrate deposits at about the same order of magnitude as all other fossil fuels combined. Over the long run, a methane outgassing-amplifier process could potentially precipitate a disastrous strong, positive feedback warming. Even if the methane from melting permafrost and decomposing clathrates were to be rapidly con-verted into carbon dioxide, the possible outcomes are still worrisome. This mechanism is one leading suspect in the so-called PETM (Paleocene–Eocene Thermal Maximum) event of some 55 million years ago when carbon diox-ide and temperatures spiked in the geological record over the course of some tens of thousands of years. The increase in carbon dioxide during the PETM is comparable to what might be attained in the course of a century or so from now under the business-as-usual burning of fossil fuels. Average world-wide surface temperatures went up during the PETM by maybe about 5 or so degrees Celsius. If it occurred at all as part of the currently unfolding climate change drama, such a large methane-release event would likely take centu-ries to materialize because the presumed initiator would be the slow-acting gradual warming of permafrost and ocean waters at the depths of the conti-nental shelves. Thus, while it is a low-probability event that might transpire only centuries from now (if at all), the possibility of a climate meltdown from bad permafrost and clathrate feedbacks is not just the outcome of a mathematical theory; it has some real physical basis. Other examples of an actual physical basis for catastrophic threshold outcomes could be cited. Fur-thermore, with geologically instantaneous massive increases in greenhouse gases, having no precedent in tens (or even perhaps hundreds) of millions of years, there is the dreaded possibility of really bad black swan climate outcomes that cannot yet be cited because no one has yet thought of them.

Suppose for the sake of argument that such an event like massive meth-ane or carbon dioxide releases with strong feedbacks began in earnest a century or so from now. In this science fiction scenario, we might then become very scared that we were riding along a trajectory leading to high-temperature increases, accompanied by relatively rapid melting or even collapse of the Greenland and West Antarctica ice sheets (or by altering ocean circulation patterns, or severely altering planet-wide precipitation patterns, and so forth). There could well be many other nasty tipping-point surprises, some of which are black swan events that we cannot now even imagine. What might we then do? In the face of rapidly rising temperatures, we might be tempted to try to deliberately geoengineer the planet as a quick fix, which would be sufficient to restore temperatures to safer levels at least temporarily while we try, this time perhaps seriously, to cut back drastically on greenhouse gas emissions and undertake more permanent, if much slower-acting, measures.

A National Academy of Sciences study defined *geoengineering* as "options that would involve large-scale engineering of our environment in order to combat or counteract the effects of changes in atmospheric chemistry." Similarly, a study of the Royal Society defined it as "the deliberate large-scale manipulation of the planetary environment to counteract anthropogenic climate change." There are several possible forms of geoengineering. But as of now, it seems that there is only one type that would offer a quick fix to the problem of increasing temperatures. This form of geoengineering would create a space sunshade by shooting reflective particles into the stratosphere that block out a small but significant fraction of incoming solar radiation.

Henceforth in this chapter, I abuse terminology by identifying the term *geoengineering* specifically with providing an artificial space sunshade. (In the literature, this is classified under "solar radiation management" as opposed to being classified under "carbon dioxide removal.") I could talk about other forms of geoengineering, but in this brief chapter, I think it is allowable and even useful to focus sharply on this one particular form. So from now on when I discuss geoengineering, I am discussing what I will call a "geoengineered sunshade."

A geoengineered sunshade of particles placed in the stratosphere introduces immense difficulties, dangers, and dilemmas of its own making, which I will touch on shortly. Almost no one is advocating this measure as a first line of defense against climate change. But it might have an important niche role as an emergency fallback component in a complete portfolio of options to deal with global warming. This may prove to be significant if, for reasons that I have already outlined, very little is done about averting climate change until the effects are visibly and tangibly bearing down on us at least as seriously as, say, a major protracted worldwide recession. Besides, consideration of a particular example in the specific form of a geoengineered sunshade may help us now to envision more concretely a possibly important set of issues that could come online a century or so from now, which, after all, is the ultimate purpose of this book.

The planet itself naturally geoengineers a temporary sunshade every time there is an explosive volcanic eruption anywhere on Earth sufficiently powerful to shoot sulfur dioxide precursors into the stratosphere. The resulting aerosol particles that coalesce around the sulfur dioxide reflect back incoming sunlight, thereby lowering Earth's surface temperatures almost immediately. The effect is rapid, if short lived, because the stratospheric aerosols decompose rapidly (and harmlessly, since there is no acid rain from the sulfur dioxide because it is in the stratosphere). The last time this naturally occurring phenomenon transpired was during the eruption of Mount Pinatubo in 1991, which was estimated to have lowered the average surface temperature of the earth by about 0.5 degrees Celsius during the subsequent year, returning to its baseline temperature thereafter.

Scientists had been well aware of this naturally geoengineered sunshade effect for a long time, along with an awareness that humans could in principle emulate this process if they wished to, even possibly improving it by substituting more effective reflective materials than sulfur-dioxide-centered aerosols. But in 2006, the Nobel Prize–winning chemist Paul Crutzen published a serious proposal that humanity should discuss openly the possible role of an artificially geoengineered sunshade in case the feeble attempts at emissions controls might in the future, as then seemed likely (and to me seems even more likely now), fail to prevent adverse climate events from occurring.[2] Crutzen had been awarded his Nobel Prize for researching the inadvertently geoengineered loss of the ozone layer from man-made chlorofluorocarbons, so he brought along high scientific and moral credibility with his proposal.

Since then, discussion about researching and investigating a geoengineered sunshade has grown enormously. It is an extraordinarily controversial idea. To repeat, almost no serious observer is advocating a geoengineered sunshade as a first line of defense against climate change.

But the fact remains that it is the only measure that can lower worldwide surface temperatures immediately, and therefore it represents the only human response that might quickly ward off the catastrophic impacts of accelerating-temperature trajectories. By comparison, carbon dioxide emissions reductions are extremely slow acting on climate change due to very long inertial lags. Even if it could be so ordained instantaneously, a complete cessation of carbon dioxide emissions would be unlikely to fend off many catastrophes by the time that they appeared. Given the magnitude of the international public goods problem involved and considering its expense and uncertainty, many (including me) reluctantly consider it unlikely that significant worldwide greenhouse gas reductions will begin in earnest until and unless the threat of dangerous climate change becomes tangible and imminent.

The other thing that a geoengineered sunshade has going for it is its unbelievably cheap cost. But is this very low cost a good thing or a bad thing? In fact, its extraordinary costlessness turns the geoengineered sunshade into a public goods nightmare of a magnitude that rivals the climate change problem itself. This twin externality dilemma may actually turn out to haunt the future of the planet.

A geoengineered sunshade has a long list of things going against it. First, it will not alleviate in the slightest any problems associated with an abnormally high concentration of carbon dioxide. Chief among these problems is ocean acidification, which would proceed apace. So the wholesale destruction of entire ocean ecosystems, including wiping out coral reefs, would be unaltered. Indeed, it could be argued that a major oceanic extinction event might even be made more likely if the world were lulled into a false sense of biosecurity from a lower global warming of surface temperatures without corresponding declines in carbon dioxide levels.

The full climatological effects of a geoengineered sunshade are highly uncertain. What little we know of what might happen comes mainly from computer simulations. These are naturally dependent on parameterizations, functional forms, and, last but not least, getting the overall structure right. Detailed prediction of regional weather patterns, such as local precipitation events, tends to be an especially weak aspect of numerical global climate models. So while we can be fairly sure that shooting reflective particles into the stratosphere will lower global surface temperatures on average, we are much more highly unsure about what will happen at various times and various locations on Earth. For many critics, the law of unintended consequences reigns supreme here. Almost for sure, precipitation patterns would be altered, perhaps greatly altered for the worse. There are also possible threats to the ozone layer. If some crucial structural elements were missing from the models, this could turn out to be yet another instance where human hubris ushered in a catastrophic black swan event. In this way of looking at things, there is a high enough chance that the cure may be worse than the disease to warrant abandoning further thinking about any such enterprise.

Even if it worked perfectly, a geoengineered sunshade is only a temporary solution in the sense that it must be continuously renewed. In the case of sulfur dioxide, the aerosol effect lasts only about a year, and so the stratosphere must be continually reseeded with sulfate particles supplied by rockets, balloons, aircraft, or whatever else. This temporary aspect could be a relatively good thing or a relatively bad thing depending on how it is viewed. On the one hand, the process could be throttled back or even stopped at any time, we hope after serious reduction of greenhouse gas emissions has been attained in the interim (although then it is an open question of how much assurance there might be that the system would return to "normal"). On the other hand, to go in the direction of stratospheric seeding is to put the planet on an addictive and potentially very dangerous drug regimen that may not be easy to stop.

Another argument frequently made against a geoengineered sunshade is that it represents a form of moral hazard problem. Seeding the stratosphere with reflective particles is extraordinarily cheap. An argument frequently made against researching or even entertaining the idea of a geoengineered sunshade is that if the public comprehends just how cheap and easy this approach might be, then the public might easily mistake it for an inexpensive "solution" to the problem of anthropogenic climate change. By this logic, even disseminating such information might well lower the political will to take the more arduous route of seriously reducing greenhouse gas emissions. So maybe it is better not to even bring up discussion of this option in the first place.

My purpose here is not to discuss in much detail the pros and cons of an engineered sunshade approach to the climate change problem. I merely want to convey the most elementary knowledge of the basic underlying issues. This approach has currently received sufficient attention that it has already generated a sizable literature, which can readily be consulted online.

By now, I think that the outlines of a scientific consensus have emerged on the role of an engineered sunshade approach to the climate change problem. Not everyone subscribes to what I am describing here as a consensus view, but enough do that I think it is worthwhile giving a rough outline before proceeding further.

Almost everyone agrees that a geoengineered sunshade is a very scary proposition with enough inherent dangers that it is vastly inferior to the more conventional strategy of cutting back severely on greenhouse gas emissions. Almost everyone also agrees that a geoengineered sunshade is likely to be a vastly less expensive way of keeping down average global temperatures than the more conventional strategy of cutting back severely on greenhouse gas emissions. More controversial is what seems like an emerging consensus that the downside risks of not doing research now (or in the near future) on a geoengineered sunshade outweighs the downside risks of undertaking now (or in the near future) early preliminary research on this option. The main argument for doing research is the one originally put forth by Paul Crutzen in 2006, which at the time it was published lacked broad support and was probably opposed by a majority of the scientific community. The argument is simple: the measures thus far undertaken to curtail greenhouse gas emissions are woefully inadequate and look as if they will be woefully inadequate into the foreseeable future. In such an eventuality, what do we turn to should future temperatures rise sharply, accompanied by what looks like the approaching danger of some form of global catastrophe? A geoengineered sunshade is the only option currently imaginable that is capable of knocking down global average temperatures in a hurry. On balance, all things being considered, is it not better to be prepared by finding out as much as possible about this option well before any temptation arises to employ it? So the argument in favor of doing research now on a geoengineered sunshade is really almost an argument by default.

I now push this argument by default even further by emphasizing that the future of a geoengineered sunshade has a certain inevitable unavoidability built into it. This inevitable unavoidability comes from the second, thus far relatively neglected, public goods aspect of this twin externality of climate change.

In a perceptive and important article, "The Incredible Economics of Geoengineering," Scott Barrett drew attention to how unbelievably cheap the economic costs of putting up and keeping in place a geoengineered sunshade would be.[3] Essentially any determined country with even a medium-sized economy could, if unopposed, put up a geoengineered sunshade on its own in answer to its own perceived need to lower global temperatures quickly.

This is a true twin externality to the conventional externality of curtailing greenhouse gases. The conventional climate change externality is the mother of all externalities because cutting back on greenhouse gases is so expensive relative to the difficulty of attaining meaningful global agreement (with international verification and compliance penalties) on the public good of minimal climate change. But then a geoengineered sunshade might be called the father of all externalities because knocking down global average temperatures is so cheap that one country can do it unilaterally to fit its own particular perceived needs, thereby imposing a dangerous "public bad" on a multitude of other nations.

Let me now move toward the culmination of my speculations on a geoengineered planet. Of course I am writing science fiction. It may well never come to pass for a variety of reasons.

The realistic side of me says that the world will likely only minimally limit greenhouse gas emissions until it is perceived that some clear and present danger of climate change is an actual threat to the average person. The mother of all externalities is too strong. The costs of a non-carbon-based technology seem high, and the extraordinary degree of international cooperation required is not there, at least not yet. The threat of climate change is just too remote, too hypothetical, too far in the distant future to compete with real problems that are present here and now. To ask people to think and act otherwise, in an international context no less, is to ask a lot of human nature.

The way I think this story will unfold, alas, is that the world will continue to emit a lot of greenhouse gases without much genuine abatement until a crisis of climate change is clearly perceived. We are in something like a Malthusian trap here. I fear that the real-world equilibrating mechanism is that greenhouse gases will pile up in the atmosphere until some clear and present climate danger appears that demands something like immediate action. The mother of all externalities will resist a serious worldwide coordinated attack on the problem until the frightening real impact (or perhaps real imminent threat) of some scary geoevent mobilizes a genuine popular groundswell of bottom-up grassroots demands for immediate action.

Enormous structural uncertainties connect emissions trajectories to the timing of what happens long afterward—including the time when direct climate threats, however they are defined, first appear. What I am saying is that the uncertainty will be resolved more on the side of the random variable time of arrival being realized given the perceived action threshold threat, rather than the other way around. In other words, define first a climate change of sufficient magnitude for the average person to demand immediate action. Then run a business-as-usual trajectory of climate change. The time when significant action is actually undertaken will be about when the uncertain trajectory attains the minimal perceived impact required for action. So the pessimistic side of me says that we will keep on piling up greenhouse gases until that unknown and uncertain future time when the trajectory of direct climate consequences crosses some immediate-action threshold.

But at just about this point, the father of all externalities kicks in. It is so cheap to unilaterally geoengineer a sunshade that it may prove irresistible for those countries that are especially hard hit by adverse climate change and whose population is demanding immediate relief. My nightmare scenario for a century or so from now is that there may be incredible tension between these two twin externalities of climate change. This could really put the future world in a bad place.

What to do about all this? I think it cannot be emphasized strongly enough that the sooner the world recognizes that a geoengineered sunshade could well turn out to be the father of all externalities, the better prepared we will be for the possible consequences. I do not think that ignoring the second twin externality of climate change is a sensible, or even a feasible, option.

First, there is desperate need for some kind of an overarching international framework to deal with issues of a geoengineered sunshade. At this stage it would be premature to speculate in what final form this might or should emerge, but preliminary meetings to discuss the problem and the issues could and should start taking place soon. The eventual aim is to develop rules and regulations along with a governance structure for determining when and how the international community might conceivably use a geoengineered sunshade. It is far too early to say what these rules and regulations might be, but it is not at all too early to air the preliminary issues that might be included in such a framework.

Simultaneously, we need to find out as much as possible as soon as possible about the science of a geoengineered sunshade, including possibly running some proof-of-concept field trials on a small scale. The moral hazard argument against researching a geoengineered sunshade is that if the public comprehends just how cheap this approach might be, then it might be seduced by an inexpensive "solution" to the problem of anthropogenic climate change. My own sense is just the opposite: if the public perceives that a geoengineered sunshade is being considered and discussed by governments in the international community, for whatever reason, the shock value is more likely to alert people to just how serious the climate change problem really is. If the father of all externalities (a geoengineered sunshade) is backing us into a corner where we must take its prospects seriously, then maybe we should be expending more effort overcoming the mother of all externalities by negotiating a serious international treaty that hammers out the details of expensive cost sharing to severely limit the world's carbon emissions.

To sum up, this is my own science fiction candidate for the world's biggest problem a century or so hence. The large-scale interbraided tension between "humanity" and "nature," which was a long time in building but whose enormous magnitude first really became apparent with what was labeled the Anthropocene epoch at the beginning of the twenty-first century, will widen and strengthen to epic proportions by the beginning of the twenty-second century. At that time there will no longer be any illusions remaining about humans "preserving" nature; the real issue will concern humans coevolving wisely with their own anthropogenic version of a forever altered nature.

The driving force in this transformation will be the tension between the twin externalities of climate change. The mother of all externalities will prove too strong to pay the price today for an expensive global public good whose payoffs are viewed by the average person as hypothetical and located in an abstract distant future. The more pressing weight of other concerns will prevent significant cutbacks being made in carbon emissions now. This situation of relative inaction will more or less continue until sufficient greenhouse gases pile up in the atmosphere over a long enough time that some clear and present climate danger appears that clearly demands something like immediate action. So the pessimistic prediction is that the current trajectory of more-or-less business as usual will continue until the frightening real impact (or perhaps just the real imminent threat) of some scary geoevent mobilizes a genuinely popular groundswell of bottom-up grassroots demands for immediate relief. When the average person feels that climate change is as immediate a threat to global welfare as, say, a deep, prolonged recession, then strong action will be seriously contemplated.

The time when such a visible climate threat threshold first appears is highly uncertain, being the realization of some incredibly complicated random variable. By this time, however, it may be too late to take effective remedial action. In any event, the father of all externalities will then make the unilateral imposition of an essentially costless geoengineered sunshade extremely tempting for any country feeling especially hard pressed by what it perceives as an intolerable threat to its own well being.

Of course, a great many currently unforeseeable developments during the next century or so could cause this nightmare express to derail and jump off its tracks. But suppose China and India continue to develop at breakneck speed, and suppose their growth momentum is joined by several other less developed countries that also aspire to taste an advanced lifestyle. Suppose the United States and Japan and several other economically advanced countries continue to drag their feet. Then I am not at all sure we can count on the deployment of a carbon-free breakthrough technology or some other miracle to rescue the situation over the next century or so.

I hope that my gloomy scenario never comes to pass. But is it not prudent to simultaneously lobby for the best and plan for the worst? The twin externality dilemma of climate change means that the international community has a lot of work cut out for it over the next century or so.

Contributors

Daron Acemoglu is Elizabeth and James Killian Professor of Economics at MIT. He is also Fellow of the American Academy of Arts and Sciences, and Fellow of the Econometric Society. He is the 2005 recipient of the John Bates Clark Medal and the author of several books, most recently *Why Nations Fail: Origins of Power, Poverty and Prosperity* (2012, with James Robinson).

Angus Deaton is the Dwight D. Eisenhower Professor of Economics and International Affairs at Princeton University. He is a Corresponding Fellow of the British Academy, a Fellow of the American Academy of Arts and Sciences and of the Econometric Society, and, in 1978, he was the first recipient of the society's Frisch Medal. He was President of the American Economic Association in 2009. He is the author of several books, most recently *The Great Escape: Health, Wealth and the Origins of Inequality* (2013).

Avinash K. Dixit is John J. F. Sherrerd '52 University Professor of Economics Emeritus at Princeton University. He has held visiting professorships at MIT and visiting scholar positions at the International Monetary Fund, the London School of Economics, the Institute for International Economic Studies (Stockholm), and the Russell Sage Foundation. He is the author of several books, most recently *The Art of Strategy: A Game-Theorist's Guide to Success in Business and Life* (2008, with Barry Nalebuff).

Edward L. Glaeser is the Fred and Eleanor Glimp Professor of Economics at Harvard, where he also serves as Director of the Taubman Center for State and Local Government and the Rappaport Institute for Greater Boston. He is a member of the American Academy of Arts and Sciences and Fellow of the Econometric Society. He is the author of several books, including *Triumph of the City* (2011).

Andreu Mas-Colell is Professor of Economics at the Universitat Pompeu Fabra, Barcelona, Spain. He is currently Minister of Economy and Knowledge of the government of Catalonia. He was President of the Econometric Society and of the European Economic Association. He is Foreign Associate of the United States National Academy of Sciences, and Foreign Honorary Member of the American Economic Association. He is the author (with Michael D. Whinston and Jerry R. Green) of *Microeconomic Theory* (1995).

Ignacio Palacios-Huerta is Professor of Management, Economics and Strategy at the London School of Economics. He has held visiting professorships at the University of Chicago and Stanford University, and was National Fellow at the Hoover Institution. He is Senior Fellow at the Ikerbasque Foundation at UPV/EHU, and is also a member of the board of directors at Athletic Club de Bilbao. He is the author of *Beautiful Game Theory* (2013).

John E. Roemer is Elizabeth S. and A. Varick Stout Professor of Political Science and Economics at Yale University. He is a Fellow of the Econometric Society, a past Guggenheim Fellow and Russell Sage Fellow, a member of the American Academy of Arts and Sciences, and a Corresponding Fellow of the British Academy.

Alvin E. Roth is the George Gund Professor of Economics and Business Administration Emeritus and the Craig and Susan McCaw Professor of Economics at Stanford University. He shared the 2012 Nobel Memorial Prize in Economics.

Robert J. Shiller is Sterling Professor of Economics at Yale University and Professor of Finance and Fellow at the International Center for Finance, Yale School of Management. His repeat-sales home price indexes, developed originally with Karl E. Case, are now published as the Standard & Poor's/ Case Shiller Home Price Indices. He is the author of several books, most recently *Finance and the Good Society* (2012), and his column, "Economic View," regularly appears in the *New York Times*.

Robert M. Solow is Professor of Economics Emeritus and Institute Professor Emeritus at MIT. He was awarded the John Bates Clark Medal in 1961 and received the 1987 Nobel Memorial Prize in Economics.

Martin L. Weitzman is Professor of Economics at Harvard University. He is also an elected Fellow of the Econometric Society and the American Academy of Arts and Sciences. He has previously worked for the World Bank, International Monetary Fund, and Environmental Protection Agency. He is the author of *Income, Wealth, and the Maximum Principle* (2003).

Notes

Chapter 1

1. See D. Acemoglu, S. Johnson, J. Robinson, and P. Yared, "Income and Democracy," *American Economic Review* 98 (2008): 808–842 on data sources and definitions. Both the Freedom House and Polity IV democracy indexes are normalized so that 0 corresponds to the least democratic and 1 corresponds to most democratic. Both figures are (unweighted) averages for balanced samples of countries: 164 for Polity IV and 186 for Freedom House. All colonies are assigned a score of 0 prior to independence, and countries that have separated are assigned the score from the united country priors of separation.

2. W. Lippmann, *Public Opinion* (New York: Free Press, 1965), 195.

3. T. Fujiwara, "Voting Technology, Political Responsiveness, and Infant Health: Evidence from Brazil" (PhD diss., University of British Columbia, 2010).

4. GDP per capita figures are from the Angus Maddison historical data set, http://www.ggdc.nl/maddison/. World GDP per capita is a population-weighted average of GDP per capita for a balanced panel of 144 countries and uses Maddison's estimates for GDP per capita for different regions for early parts of the sample. The same data are also used in figures 1.3 and 1.11.

5. D. Acemoglu, S. Johnson, and J. Robinson, "Reversal of Fortune: Geography and Institutions in the Making of the Modern World Income Distribution," *Quarterly Journal of Economics* 117 (2002): 1231–1294.

6. See D. Autor, F. Levy, and R. Murnane, "The Skill Content of Recent Technological Change: An Empirical Exploration," *Quarterly Journal of Economics* 118 (2003): 1279–1334, and Acemoglu and Autor, "Skills, Tasks and Technologies: Implications for Employment Earnings" in O. Ashenfelter and D. Card (eds.), *The Handbook of Labor Economics*, vol. 4b, Elsevier, Amsterdam, 1043–1171.

7. See Acemoglu and Autor, "Skills, Tasks and Technologies." Both figures are for the weekly earnings of full-time (male and female) workers between the ages of sixteen and sixty-four. Figure 1.4 uses data from the March Current Population Surveys

(CPS). The percentiles are estimated using the CPS weights, and wages are converted to real terms using the personal consumption expenditure deflator. Figure 1.5 uses the Census and American Community Survey (ACS) sample of full-time workers for the years 1970 and 2008, respectively. The percentiles are estimated for weekly real wages using the Census/ACS weights.

8. See D. Acemoglu and S. Johnson, S 2007, "Disease and Development: The Effect of Life Expectancy on Economic Growth," *Journal of Political Economy* 115: 925–985 for data sources. The numbers shown are unweighted averages with missing data interpolated using a constant growth rate.

9. The figure shows the value of exports plus imports to GDP at the world level. Data for 1870 to 1939 are from A. Estevadeordal, B. Frantz, and A. Taylor, "The Rise and Fall of World Trade, 1870–1939," *Quarterly Journal of Economics* 118 (2003): 359–407. Data for 1945 onward are from the IMF International Financial Statistics: http://elibrary-data.imf.org/. The value of exports plus imports is converted to constant dollars using the deflators provided by the IMF, and world GDP figures from Maddison are used to calculate the trade to GDP ratio.

10. These figures are constructed using the best estimates from the PRIO-UPSALA data set from B. Lacina and N. Gleditsch, "Monitoring Trends in Global Combat: A New Dataset of Battle Deaths," *European Journal of Population* 21 (2005): 145–166. International battle deaths are those recorded in conflicts between two or more recognized states. Civil war deaths are those recorded in conflicts that are fought within state borders between a government and nongovernment forces (civil war) or two nongovernment forces.

11. Steven Pinker also emphasizes these trends; see S. Pinker, *The Better Angels of Our Nature: Why Violence Has Declined* (New York: Viking Press, 2011).

12. Murder rates are constructed using the World Health Organization (WHO) data set on causes of death, http://www.who.int/healthinfo/statistics/mortality/en/index.html. The WHO reports homicide rates (excluding war casualties) from country reports for a set of sixteen western European countries, the United States, Canada, New Zealand, and Australia. Missing data for 8 observations are interpolated using a constant growth rate, and the regional trend in homicide rates is used to construct estimates for 39 observations (out of a total of 1,120 observations).

13. U.N. population projections from http://www.who.int/healthinfo/statistics/mortality/en/index.html.

14. Commodity prices are from the U.S. Geological Survey, http://www.who.int/healthinfo/statistics/mortality/en/index.html. All prices are in constant dollars and are normalized to 100 in 1980.

15. See D. Acemoglu and J. Robinson, *Why Nations Fail: The Origins of Power, Prosperity and Poverty* (New York: Crown, 2012).

16. D. Acemoglu, S. Johnson, J. Robinson, and P. Yared, "Income and Democracy," *American Economic Review* 98 (2008): 808–842.

17. Acemoglu and Robinson, *Why Nations Fail*, chap. 9.

18. D. Acemoglu, P. Aghion, and F. Zilibotti, "Distance to Frontier, Selection, and Economic Growth," *Journal of the European Economic Association* 4 (2006): 37–74.

19. J. Snyder, *The Myths of Empire: Domestic Politics and International Ambition* (Ithaca, NY: Cornell University Press, 1993).

20. C. Murray, *Coming Apart: The State of White America, 1960–2010* (New York: Crown 2012).

21. D. Acemoglu, "Directed Technical Change," *Review of Economic Studies* 69 (2002): 781–809.

22. W. Hanlon, "Necessity Is the Mother of Innovation: Input Supplies and Directed Technical Change," PhD diss., Columbia University, 2011.

23. D. Acemoglu, and J. Linn, "Market Size in Innovation: Theory and Evidence from the Pharmaceutical Industry," *Quarterly Journal of Economics* 119 (2004): 1049–1090.

24. D. Acemoglu and S. Johnson, "Disease and Development: The Effect of Life Expectancy on Economic Growth," *Journal of Political Economy* 115 (2007): 925–985.

25. E. Meyersson, "Islamic Rule and the Emancipation of the Poor and Pious," working paper, London School of Economics (2011).

26. World emissions and concentration levels are taken from the Carbon Dioxide Information Analysis Center (CDIAC); see http://cdiac.ornl.gov/trends/emis/ overview_2008.html and http://cdiac.ornl.gov/trends/co2/. Emissions are plotted in equivalent carbon dioxide billion metric tons. Carbon dioxide concentration levels in the atmosphere are from two sources. Data for 1900–1959 come from measurements in ice cores in Law Dome, Antarctica. Data for 1960–2010 come from in situ air samples taken collected at Mauna Loa, Hawaii.

27. D. Acemoglu, P. Aghion, L. Bursztin, and D. Hemous, "The Environment and Directed Technical Change," *American Economic Review* 102 (2012): 131–166.

Chapter 3

1. The huge magnitudes are a sad consequence of the inflation that will have taken place over the coming century.

2. See David S. Landes, *The Wealth and Poverty of Nations* (New York: Norton, 1998), chap. 21.

3. Boston Consulting Group, "Made (Again) in the USA: The Return of American Manufacturing" (August 2011), http://www.bcg.com/documents/file84471.pdf.

4. "Chile's Economy: Stimulating," *Economist,* February 19, 2009.

5. Christopher Drew, "Why Science Majors Change Their Minds (It's Just So Darn Hard)," *New York Times,* November 4, 2011.

6. Milton Friedman, *Capitalism and Freedom* (Chicago: University of Chicago Press, 1962), chap. 12.

7. Herbert Spencer, "State Tamperings with Money and Banks," in his *Essays: Scientific, Political, and Speculative* (New York: D. Appleton & Co., 1891), 354.

8. See "The Darwin Awards: In Search of Smart" (February 22, 2013), http://www.darwinawards.com/.

9. To state the difference rigorously, what Keynes said can be written in formal terms as: "There exists a time T such that for every person X, X is dead at T," when he should have said, "For every person X, there exists a time T(X) such that X is dead at T(X)." Keynes's dictum would apply to a complete nuclear holocaust, but thankfully that seems a remote possibility now.

10. Robert Frank, *Richistan: A Journey through the American Wealth Boom and the Lives of the New Rich* (New York: Crown, 2007).

11. Mancur Olson, *The Rise and Decline of Nations: Economic Growth, Stagflation, and Social Rigidities* (New Haven, CT: Yale University Press, 1982).

Chapter 4

1. http://pewresearch.org/?p=2037/poll-obama-approval-state-of-economy-national-conditions-personal-financial-situation.

2. John Galbraith's *The Affluent Society* (New York: New American Library, 1958) similarly overestimates the extent to which Americans would enjoy increasing wealth in the form of leisure.

3. R. Solow, "Technical Change and the Aggregate Production Function," *Review of Economics and Statistics* 39, no. 3 (1957): 312–320.

4. Chang-Tai Hsieh and Ralph Ossa, "A Global View of Productivity Growth in China," NBER working paper 16778 (2011).

5. Chinhui Juhn and Simon Potter, "Changes in Labor Force Participation in the United States," *Journal of Economic Perspectives* 20, no. 3 (2006): 27–46.

6. Michael Hout and Caroline Hanley, "The Overworked American Family: Trends and Nontrends in Working Hours, 1968–2001: A Century of Difference," University of California, Berkeley, working paper (2002).

7. Suzanne M. Bianchi, Melissa A. Milkie, Liana C. Sayer, and John P. Robinson, "Is Anyone Doing the Housework? Trends in the Gender Division of Household Labor," *Social Forces* 79 (2000): 191–228.

8. Over the same period, married men increased their time on these activities only from 1.5 to 1.9 hours per week.

9. Robert J. Barro, "Determinants of Democracy," *Journal of Political Economy* 107 (1999): 158–183.

10. Daron Acemoglu, Simon Johnson, James A. Robinson, and Pierre Yared, "Income and Democracy," *American Economic Review* 98 (2008): 808–842 presents an alternative view supported by the fact that changes in income are not strongly associated with changes in democracy.

11. E. L. Glaeser, G. A. M. Ponzetto, and A. Shleifer, "Why Does Democracy Need Education?" *Journal of Economic Growth* 12, no. 2 (2007): 77–99.

12. Xavier Sala-i-Martin, "The World Distribution of Income (Estimated from Individual Country Distributions)," NBER working paper 8933 (2002).

13. Claudia Goldin and Robert A. Margo, "The Great Compression: The Wage Structure in the United States at Mid-Century," *Quarterly Journal of Economics* 107 (1992): 1–34.

14. Chinhui Juhn and Simon Potter, "Changes in Labor Force Participation in the United States," *Journal of Economic Perspectives* 20, no. 3 (2006): 27–46.

15. David G. Blanchflower and Andrew J. Oswald, "Well-Being over Time in Britain and the USA," *Journal of Public Economics* 88 (2004): 1359–1386.

16. A. Abdulkadiroglu, J. Angrist, S. R. Cohodes, S. Dynarski, J. Fullerton, T. J. Kane, and P. Pathak, *Informing the Debate: Comparing Boston's Charter, Pilot, and Traditional Schools* (Boston: Boston Foundation, 2009).

17. Raj Chetty, John N. Friedman, and Jonah E. Rockoff, "The Long-Term Impacts of Teachers: Teacher Value-Added and Student Outcomes in Adulthood," NBER Working Paper 17699 (2011).

18. Martin Daly, Margo Wilson, and Shawn Vasdev, "Income Inequality and Homicide Rates in Canada and the United States," *Canadian Journal of Criminology* 43, no. 2 (2001): 219–236.

19. E. F. P. Luttmer, "Neighbors as Negatives: Relative Earnings and Well-Being," *Quarterly Journal of Economics* 120 (2005): 963–1002.

20. David M. Cutler, Edward L. Glaeser, and Jesse M. Shapiro, "Why Have Americans Become More Obese?" *Journal of Economic Perspectives* 17 (2003): 93–118.

21. Darius Lakdawalla and Tomas Philipson, "The Growth of Obesity and Technological Change: A Theoretical and Empirical Examination," NBER working paper 8946 (2002).

22. http://www.cdc.gov/NCHS/data/hestat/obesity_adult_07_08/obesity_adult _07_08.pdf.

23. L. B. Finer, "Trends in Premarital Sex in the United States, 1954–2003," *Public Health Report* 122, no. 1 (2007): 73–78.

24. Andrew M. Greeley, Robert T. Michael, and Tom W. Smith, "Americans and Their Sexual Partners," *Society* 27 (1990): 36–42.

25. Betsey Stevenson and Justin Wolfers, "Marriage and Divorce: Changes and Their Driving Forces," *Journal of Economic Perspectives* 21, no. 2 (2007): 27–52.

26. John H. Johnson and Christopher J. Mazingo, "The Economic Consequences of Unilateral Divorce for Children," University of Illinois CBA Office of Research working paper 00–0112 (2000).

27. Steven Pinker, *The Better Angels of Our Nature: Why Violence Has Declined* (New York: Viking Press, 2011).

28. Edward L. Glaeser, "The Political Economy of Hatred," *Quarterly Journal of Economics* 120, no. 1 (2005): 45–86.

29. Matthew Gentzkow and Jesse M. Shapiro, "Ideological Segregation Online and Offline," *Quarterly Journal of Economics* 126 (2011): 1799–1839.

30. J. M. Twenge and S. T. Campbell, "Generational Differences in Psychological Traits and Their Impact on the Workplace," *Journal of Managerial Psychology* 29 (2008): 862–877.

31. K. H. Trzesniewski and M. B. Donnellan, "Rethinking 'Generation Me': A Study of Cohort Effects from 1976 to 2006," *Perspectives in Psychological Science* 5 (2010): 58–75.

32. http://psycnet.apa.org/index.cfm?fa=buy.optionToBuy&id=2011-05681-001.

33. Robert D. Putnam, *Bowling Alone: The Collapse and Revival of American Community* (New York: Simon & Schuster, 2000).

34. Matthew E. Kahn, "The Death Toll from Natural Disasters: The Role of Income, Geography and Institutions," *Review of Economics and Statistics* 87 (2005): 271–284.

35. William Rosen, *Justinian's Flea: Plague, Empire, and the Birth of Europe* (New York: Viking Press, 2007).

36. Werner Troesken, "Typhoid Rates and the Public Acquisition of Private Waterworks, 1880–1920," *Journal of Economic History* 59 (1999): 927–948.

37. Paul R. Ehrlich, *The Population Bomb* (New York: Ballantine Books, 1968).

38. Amartya Sen, *Poverty and Famines: An Essay on Entitlement and Deprivation* (Oxford: Clarendon Press, 1981).

39. Stephen Devereux, "Famine in the Twentieth Century," Institute of Development Studies working paper (2000).

40. Dana Cordell, Jan-Olof Drangert, and Stuart Whit, "The Story of Phosphorus: Global Food Security and Food for Thought," *Global Environmental Change* 19 (2009): 292–305.

41. ftp://ftp.bls.gov/pub/special.requests/ce/share/2010/higherincome.txt.

42. http://www.whitehouse.gov/sites/default/files/omb/budget/fy2013/assets/hist03z2.xls.

43. Alberto Alesina and Edward L. Glaeser, *Fighting Poverty in the U.S. and Europe: A World of Difference* (New York: Oxford University Press, 2004).

44. Raquel Fernandez and Dani Rodrik, "Resistance to Reform: Status Quo Bias in the Presence of Individual-Specific Uncertainty," *American Economic Review* 81 (1991): 1146–1155.

45. Paul Romer, "Preferences, Promises, and the Politics of Entitlement," in *Individual and Social Responsibility: Child Care, Education, Medical Care, and Long-Term Care in America*, ed. Victor T. Fuchs, 195–220 (Chicago: University of Chicago Press, 1996).

46. Edward L. Glaeser, "The Political Economy of Hatred." *Quarterly Journal of Economics* 120, no. 1 (2005): 45–86.

47. Edward L. Glaeser, Joseph Gyourko, and Raven E. Saks, "Why Have Housing Prices Gone Up?" Harvard Institute of Economic Research working paper 2061 (2005).

48. Edward L. Glaeser and Bryce A. Ward, "The Causes and Consequences of Land Use Regulation: Evidence from Greater Boston," *Journal of Urban Economics* 65 (2008): 265–278.

49. Edward L. Glaeser, J. Gyourko, and R. E. Saks, "Why Is Manhattan So Expensive? Regulation and the Rise in House Prices," *Journal of Law and Economics* 48 (2005): 331–370.

50. Marianne Bertrand and Francis Kramarz, "Does Entry Regulation Hinder Job Creation? Evidence from the French Retail Industry," *Quarterly Journal of Economics* 117 (2002): 1369–1414.

Chapter 5

1. See S. Almenar Palau, "La recepción e influencia de Keynes y del keynesianismo en España (I): 1919–1936," in *Economía y Economistas Españoles*, vol. 6, ed. E. Fuentes-Quintana, 783–851 (Galaxia Gutemberg-Funcas, Madrid, 2001); E. Fuentes-

Quintana, "John Maynard Keynes en España," *Papeles de Economia Española* 17 (1983): 237–334; J. Velarde Fuertes, "Biblioteca hispana de Marx, Keynes y Schumpeter. Una primera aproximación," *Papeles de Economía Española* 17 (1983): 374–416; and J. Velarde Fuertes, "Keynes en España," in *La herencia de Keynes,* ed. Rubio de Urquia (Alianza Universidad, Madrid, 1988).

2. The trend in developed countries is to decrease population, while from 2050, population growth in emerging countries is expected to slow down. See A. Madison, *The World Economy: A Millennial Perspective* (Paris: OECD, 2001), and United Nations, *World Population Prospects: The 2006 Revision* (New York: United Nations, 2006).

3. T. Hobbes, *Leviathan* (New York: Oxford University Press, 1998).

4. On these issues, see D. M. Cutler, *Are the Benefits of Medicine Worth What We Pay for It?* Syracuse University policy brief 27 (2004) or *Your Money or Your Life* (New York: Oxford University Press, 2004). From other angles, see E. Sheshinski, *The Economic Theory of Annuities* (Princeton, NJ: Princeton University Press, 2008); A. Balaz, A. Bogojevic, and R. Karapandza, "Consequences of Increased Longevity for Wealth, Fertility, and Population Growth," *Physica A* 387 (2008), 543–550; and J. Vijg and J. Campisi, "Puzzles, Promises and a Cure for Ageing," *Nature* 454 (2008): 1065–1071.

5. On economic growth, see R. J. Barro and X. Sala-i-Martin, *Economic Growth,* 2nd ed. (Cambridge, MA: MIT Press, 2003).

6. See, for example, Q. Schiermeier, J. Tollefson, T. Scully, A. Witza, and O. Morton, "Energy Alternatives: Electricity without Carbon," *Nature* 454 (2008), 816–823.

7. See Intergovernmental Panel on Climate Change, *Synthesis Report* (Cambridge: Cambridge University Press, 2001); N. Stern, *The Economics of Climate Change* (Cambridge: Cambridge University Press, 2007); W. Nordhaus, *A Question of Balance* (New Haven, CT: Yale University Press, 2008); H. Llavador, J. Roemer, and J. Silvestre, "A Dynamic Analysis of Human Welfare in a Warming Planet," Cowles discussion paper 1673 (2008).

8. See C. Camerer, *Behavioral Game Theory: Experiments in Strategic Interaction* (Princeton, NJ: Princeton University Press, 2003); C. Camerer, G. Loewenstein, and M. Rabin, eds., *Advances in Behavioral Economics* (Princeton, NJ: Princeton University Press, 2004).

9. See, for example, D. A. Schkade and D. Kahneman, "Does Living in California Make People Happy? A Focusing Illusion in Judgments of Life Satisfaction," *Psychological Science* 9 (1998): 340–346.

10. W. J. Baumol and W. Bowen, *Performing Arts: The Economic Dilemma* (Cambridge, MA: MIT Press, 1996).

11. See C. M. Tiebout, "A Pure Theory of Local Expenditures," *Journal of Political Economy* 64 (1956): 416–424. In the Tiebout model individuals enjoy perfect mobility,

have perfect information, and are free to choose their communities. Given that they have different valuations of public services and varying abilities to pay taxes, they move across communities. This process sorts people into "optimal" communities and determines the equilibrium provision of local public goods according to their tastes.

12. On this, see C. Mann, *1491* (New York: Random House, 2005).

13. D. Warsh, "Frame Tale," *Economic Principals*, (10/11/08), www.economicprincipals .com.

Chapter 6

1. What explains the fact that roughly half the citizenry support a political party whose economic platform is only in the interests of the very richest echelon of the society? I believe the Republican party has primarily remained a national player by exploiting racism. If the distribution of party allegiance among white male voters were the same as that distribution among the rest of the polity, today's Republican party would not win elections. See J. Roemer, W. Lee, and K. van der Straeten, *Racism, Xenophobia and Distribution: Multi-Issue Politics in Advanced Democracies* (Cambridge, MA: Harvard University Press and Russell Sage Foundation, 2007), for an analysis of the effect of racism on Republican strength and on economic policy. In addition, one cannot discount the effect of private money in politics, recently extended by the Supreme Court's decision in *Citizens United* v. *FEC*. Here, the United States differs sharply from European practice.

2. Indeed, the ranks of climate skeptics among scientists are becoming very thin. See "The Conversion of a Climate Skeptic," *New York Times*, July 30, 2012, 17.

3. J. Heckman and P. LaFontaine, "The American High School Graduation Rate: Trends and Levels," IZA discussion paper 3216 (2007), http://ftp.iza.org/dp3216.pdf.

4. A. Atkinson, T. Piketty, and E. Saez, "Top Incomes in the Long Run of History," *Journal of Economic Literature* 49 (2011): 3–71.

5. H. Llavador, J. Roemer, and J. Silvestre, "North-South Convergence and the Allocation of CO^2 Emissions," Economics Working Paper 1234 (2010), Department of Economics and Business, Universitat Pompeu Fabra.

Chapter 7

1. For overviews, see Alvin E. Roth, "The Economist as Engineer: Game Theory, Experimental Economics and Computation as Tools of Design Economics," *Econometrica* 70 (2002): 1341–1378, and "What Have We Learned from Market Design?" *Economic Journal* 118 (2008): 285–310.

2. Alvin E. Roth, "Repugnance as a Constraint on Markets," *Journal of Economic Perspectives* 21, no. 3 (2007): 37–58, and Stephen Leider and Alvin E. Roth, "Kidneys for Sale: Who Disapproves, and Why?," *American Journal of Transplantation* 10, no. 5 (2010), 1221–1227.

3. John Maynard Keynes, "Economic Possibilities for Our Grandchildren," in *Essays in Persuasion* (New York: Norton, 1930), Leider and Roth, "Kidneys for Sale."

Chapter 8

1. Jared Diamond, *Collapse: How Societies Choose to Fail or Succeed* (New York: Viking, 2005); Charles C. Mann, *1491: New Revelations of the Americas before Columbus* (New York: Vintage Books, 2006).

2. Robert J. Shiller, *Macro Markets: Creating Institutions for Managing Society's Largest Economic Risks* (New York: Oxford University Press, 1993); *The New Financial Order: Risk in the Twenty-First Century* (Princeton, NJ: Princeton University Press, 2003); and *Finance and the Good Society* (Princeton, NJ: Princeton University Press, 2012).

3. See Ray Kurzweil, *The Age of Intelligent Machines* (Cambridge, MA: MIT Press, 1992), and *The Age of Spiritual Machines* (New York: Viking Press, 1999).

4. Émile Durkheim, *De la division du travail social* (Paris: Les Presses Universitaires de France, 1893); Maurice Halbwachs, *La mémoire collective* (Paris: Les Presses Universitaires de France, 1967).

5. I have been advocating GDP-linked securities for years. See Shiller, *Macro Markets*. Also see Mark J. Kamstra and Robert J. Shiller, "Trills instead of T Bills: It's Time to Replace Part of Government Debt with Shares in GDP," *Economists' Voice* (2010), http://www.markkamstra.com/papers/Economists-Voice-TrillsInsteadofTBills.pdf.

6. Milton Friedman, *Capitalism and Freedom* (Chicago: University of Chicago Press, 1963).

7. Paul Kennedy, *The Parliament of Man: The Past, Present and Future of the United Nations* (New York: Vintage, 2007).

8. Shiller, *The New Financial Order*.

9. Richard Lugar, "The Lugar Survey on Proliferation Threats and Responses" (2004), http://mx1.nuclearfiles.com/menu/key-issues/nuclear-weapons/issues/proliferation/fuel-cycle/senate-dot-gov_NPSurvey.pdf. See also Hermes L. Marganos, Kathleen Leslie, Andrew J. Tobin, Mark Adams, Steve Atkins, Nigel Miller, Angus Tucker, Risto Talas, Peter A. Walker, and Paul Culham, "War Risks and Terrorism: Insurance Institute of London Research Study Group Report 258" (London: Insurance Institute of London, 2007), and National Commission on Terrorist Attacks upon the United States, *The 9/11 Commission Report* (New York: Norton, 2004).

10. Howard C. Kunreuther and Erwann O. Michel-Kerjan, "Evaluating the Effectiveness of Terrorism Risk Financing Solutions," National Bureau of Economic Research working paper 13359 (October 2007).

11. Dwight Jaffee, Howard Kunreuther, and Erwann Michel-Kerjan, "Long Term Insurance (LTI) for Addressing Catastrophe Risk," National Bureau of Economic Research working paper w14210 (August 2008). See also Howard Kunreuther, Mark V. Pauly, and Stacey McMorrow, *Insurance and Behavioral Economics: Improving Decisions in the Most Misunderstood Industry* (Cambridge: Cambridge University Press, 2013).

12. Shiller, *The New Financial Order.*

13. Norbert Wiener, *Cybernetics, or Control and Communication in the Animal and the Machine* (New York: Wiley, 1948), 36–38.

14. Wassily Leontief, 1983 (quoted in Hallak and Caillods, *Educational Planning: The International Dimension*), referring to 3–4.

15. Jeremy Rifkin, *The End of Work: The Decline of the Global Labor Force and the Dawn of the Post-Market Era* (New York: J. P. Tarcher, 1996), 5.

Chapter 10

1. Clathrates (or hydrates) are methane molecules that are boxed into a semistable state by being surrounded by water molecules under high pressure and low temperatures. For more about methane clathrates, see the references cited in Natalia Shakhova, Igor Semiletov, Anatoly Salyuk, Vladimir Yusupov, Denis Kosmach, and Örjan Gustafsson, "Extensive Methane Venting to the Atmosphere from Sediments of the East Siberian Arctic Shelf," *Science* 327 (5970): 1246–1250.

2. Paul J. Crutzen, "Albedo Enhancement by Stratospheric Sulfur Injections: A Contribution to Resolve a Policy Dilemma?" *Climate Change* 77 (2006): 211–219.

3. Scott Barrett, "The Incredible Economics of Geoengineering," *Environmental and Resource Economics* 39 (2008): 45–54. See also the extensive references to geoengineering cited in this article.

Index

Note: Page numbers of graphs and tables are listed in italics.